Loren B. Mead

Transforming Congregations for the Future

An Alban Institute Publication

The Publications Program of The Alban Institute is assisted by a grant from Trinity Church, New York City.

Library of Congress Catalog Card Number 93-74587
ISBN 1-56699-126-9

In gratitude to four of
my teachers

Miss Carrie Cain,
Pinopolis
Terry Holmes,
Nashota and Sewanee
Andy Penick,
Chapel Hill
Verna Dozier,
Washington

Each pushed me
further than I wanted
to go.

CONTENTS

INTRODUCTION

Everyone I know who works in churches knows there is trouble. Churches do not "work" the way they used to. Roles of leadership have become more confusing and frustrating to those who hold them. What we remember as being crystal clear in church life a generation or two ago now seems muddy, uncertain.

What has gone wrong? many wonder. Who is to blame? The strong, confident, even triumphant institution that they remember from their youth--or that others tell them about from just a few decades ago— is not what they or their children experience in church today. They now see an institution exuding self-doubt, with leaders who seem less able to lead than to mimic the least common denominator of public opinion. Their vision of prophetic justice sounds suspiciously like the latest liberal definition of political correctness.

Church people talk about membership losses and cast covetous eyes at the burgeoning membership rolls of other churches that have a different theological stance or seem better at reading the market. Without a clear sense of what they ought to do, they have grown unsure that what they are doing is the right thing. If you are not sure of what you should be up to, then why not do whatever is selling best?

The people I talk to are not terribly confident as they voice these concerns. They know that these questions are not in a league with those about peace and war and justice. Yet what's happening to the church is something that touches them very deeply. It's easier to get more exercised about and involved in local church issues than about Bosnia or Somalia. Their concern about their congregations—in today's language —is not politically correct, but it matters a lot.

It matters a lot. A simple statement with deep roots. Religious
congregations do matter. They matter personally to millions of people
who find a source of meaning in a congregation. They matter to those
who week by week make their way to their religious observances and
contribute more money to churches than to any other set of institutions in
the country. They matter to those who take the values learned in those
congregations into their business relationships and continue to make
possible an economic system that is dependent upon promises and the
keeping of one's word. They matter to those who work hard to build
caring relationships—in traditional families and in new forms of community. They matter to those who build towns or counties or nations that do
what is right for most people–without being coercive to those without
power. They matter to those who care about the development of the next
generation of the young–those in families and those who have no families.

People raised in religious congregations make this a society that
cares about justice, although it often falls short. People raised in religious congregations make this a society that recognizes a responsibility
in Bosnia and Somalia, although we may be confused about precisely
what we ought to do there. People raised in religious congregations help
us have a healthy skepticism about human perfection, reminding us of
how our own society has permitted practices leading to near genocide
of Native Americans, condoning African-American slavery for more
than two centuries, exiling Japanese-American citizens to concentration
camps, and allowing radioactive experimentation on other citizens. Religious congregations condition us to ask questions of right and wrong
about public policy. Through our history the first questions about injustice often have been raised in congregations. After attempts to justify
injustice as God's will, those congregations led us to debate and finally
reject the practices.

Congregations have power and that power can have enormously
creative influence in leading us toward an ever-more humane society.
Critics and observers of American society since deToqueville have noted
this role of congregations. We do well to remember, however, that they
do have demonic potential. Congregations can care and teach us to care,
but they can also be places where prejudices are nourished and grudges
passed along to future generations.

Yes, congregations have power, enormous power. They matter. I do not plan to argue this point further, but you deserve to know that I start with this assumption.

Against this background, the fact that our churches and the congregations that make them up are in trouble is a concern not just to the religious community. It is a matter of concern for the health of the society itself.

In this book I contend that the storm buffeting the churches is very serious indeed. Much more serious than we have admitted to ourselves, and much more serious than our leaders have yet comprehended. The problems are not minor, calling for adjustments or corrections. They are problems that go to the roots of our institutions themselves. What I am describing here is not something we will fix. It is a state of existence in which we must learn to live even as we seek new directions for faithful response.

In my earlier book *The Once and Future Church,*[1] I explored some reasons for our being where we are. In my subsequent book *More Than Numbers,*[2] I gave perspectives about and tools for congregations in this time between two ages. In this book I want to take up the argument of *The Once and Future Church* and push further ahead, delving deeper into the nature of the storm we are in and making suggestions for the future. Everything I say has been influenced by the hundreds of people who have worked with me in conferences and corresponded with me. Many have asked questions or given me feedback, making points I had never thought about. I can therefore claim little in these pages as being original with me.

In chapter 1 I begin with a discussion of the serious storm I see buffeting the churches. The storm is so serious, I believe, that it marks the end of "business as usual" for the churches and marks a need for us to begin again building church from the ground up.

The heart of my argument will be in chapters 2 and 3, in which I begin to restate for our time the basic functions of congregations—what the religious enterprise in congregations is really about. I will give the best clues I have about the process that is at the heart of congregational life—a process I call transformation. I am aware that I am calling for a radically different understanding of mission, of evangelism, and of how individual congregational members are called to live it out.

That is followed by a chapter about the implications for regional judicatories and a chapter that identifies roadblocks in and guideposts on the road ahead. I have tried to include practical suggestions throughout. The first appendix is an educational design I use to help people work on some of these ideas. The second appendix gives the raw data for the graphs I use.

If my final chapter feels sermonic, forgive me. I deeply believe that the storm we are in presents the greatest opportunity the churches and religious leaders have ever had. Bar none. I also believe it is a deeper challenge and threat than religious leaders have faced in many centuries. We are in serious trouble that we will not get out of soon or easily. When we get clear of this storm, our religious institutions may bear little resemblance to those with which we grew up.

I have two other comments about what I am doing and why. In my books I have never used much of the language usually found in theological works. Some readers have complained that I am not adequately "theological" in my approach. That particular criticism confounds me. The substance of my concern and my method are both firmly based in a deep theological framework, but I approach things inductively, doing theology, as Terry Holmes and I used to describe it, "from the ground up." In another context, I described the way I work and think as "operational theology."[3] I do not plan to change that approach now, but I apologize if my language about congregations does not fulfill your expectations. In this book I am inviting you to do ecclesiology "from the ground up."

Finally, I want to invite you into this book as into a conversation. You know things I do not know, and I beg you to bring your knowledge to the table. Let your ideas work with mine, test them, argue with them. I know I have a limited point of view and that you have much to add. My insights come out of my life experience and bear the values and limits of their origin. Although I wrote *The Once and Future Church* out of my own experience (primarily mainline Protestant), I was delighted that so many from very different backgrounds found it helpful. Those who have found it most helpful did what I hoped they would do: They translated it into their own situations; they used it to ignite questions they had about their own congregations. I have had rabbis tell me how helpful my use of the term *Christendom* was to them in understanding the relationship of their congregations to their world. Pastors of independent congregations have told me about the "connectionalism" they discovered among congregations that were technically "nonconnectional."

So join me in a conversation. I hope that what I have to say out of my life, experience, and commitments will help you illuminate points of your life, experience, and commitments. My experience will not tell you what to do, but you can hold your experience up to mine, test my ideas to see how they translate—or if they translate. If you do that work, I think our conversation will help you discover things that should be on your agenda.

I speak out of my own faith, too. I often use words of that faith because they are how I know to express what I perceive to be true. I have tried not to use language that will offend those of other faith positions, but I have not tried to homogenize my language to do so. If my words do cause offense to your way of understanding or speaking your truth, I ask two things of you—that you accept my apology for any insensitivity and that you go back to what offended you and try to reach through the words to what I am trying to say.

I deeply believe God calls us severally to move into the future. I believe we need one another if we are to hear our own call clearly. We hear best in dialogue with one another as well as with God. I will say what I mean as clearly as I can, but I know that my vision is distorted, no matter how hard I try. I hope you will discover things I do not know as you interact with what I have to say. I hope you will discover things you did not know. For both of us this dialogue is likely to hold surprises. This is intrinsic, I believe, in the process of revelation.

This is not an optimistic book. I see much that is difficult ahead of us. I do, however, speak from a deep and abiding hope. The faith I learned in a congregation in South Carolina in the 1930s is desperately needed in the 2030s. That faith has been built up and transformed by life experiences, by relationships, and by learning, but in many ways its basics are unchanged. But the faith I received in the thirties was clothed in a world view of a now-past age, and its institutional "delivery system" reflected that age's understanding of how to do things. The institutional forms in which I learned faith and the structures for carrying it on have been hard to change. Many of them continue as today's structures, although they stopped working in some places years ago. Many of us have worked hard to reinvent those forms—with mixed success.

God calls us to a daunting task: to take those structures and those resources of faith and re-present them in forms that will carry them into the next century. I am astonished that God would invite us into such a task of co-creation. God obviously sees potential in us that we have a hard time accepting. And I believe that potential can be approached only as we in our differences enter into dialogue with each other. This book is my attempt to work at that task.

Loren B. Mead
Washington
Ash Wednesday, 1994.

CHAPTER 1

The Storm We Are In: It's Worse Than We Thought

The Storm about Numbers: Membership Losses

Those in what have been called mainline churches are feeling particularly defensive and sensitive about membership losses. Fast-growing congregations and denominations look on the traditional bellwethers—Methodist, Lutheran, Episcopal, Presbyterian, Congregational—and say, "Main? More like sideline these days." Mainliners wince. Sometimes we try to kid ourselves about the numbers by talking about how we think they've "bottomed out."

Reasons for the declines are as numerous as the commentators. I have heard reasons ranging from "its because of all the social ministries the mainline got involved in in the sixties" to "it's because the mainline is not as aggressive in its social ministries as it was in the sixties." The polarization between social liberals and conservatives plays itself out in this debate—with conservatives seeing the problem as too much liberalism and the liberals seeing the problem as too much conservatism. Each side accuses the other of divisiveness.

"Too much concern for political correctness," scoffs the conservative. "That's why everybody is leaving!"

"Fascist pietism," accuses the liberal, "turns off the people who want to make a difference at this point of historic change."

Respected researchers state that the church-membership losses illustrate a universal law of American religion: Sect-like religions sells; church-like religion dies. Their critics reply, loosely translated, "Horsehockey." (I am sure you can recognize the high intellectual level of and deep philosophical basis for this debate.)

It is hard to get clear data that is not filtered through someone's ideological presuppositions. It is also clear that "church numbers" is a fluid crap game. Many people consider themselves "members" but are not listed in the church statistics. Many people feel free to tell a census report or survey recorder that they are Presbyterians or Catholics, but they have never happened to mention it to the local Presbyterian or Catholic church! Kirk Hadaway, research officer for the United Church of Christ, has a felicitous name for the group: "mental members"![1] More recent research by Hadaway and his colleague Penny Marler of Samford University indicated that perhaps only half of the people who tell pollsters they go to church actually show up on Sunday. So we are in a land of much data, some of it conflicting, much of it closely touched by strong biases in interpretation. Further, words such as *member* and *attender* have ambiguous meanings. In our work we have located people who never darken the church doors, but they have strong emotional ties to a congregation or denomination for which they care a great deal. Still others somehow crept onto the church rolls and simply do not care a fig about the church. A number of these people, for reasons of church administration, have been taken off the rolls. Some who are on probably ought to be taken off, and some who are off probably still ought to be on. Some, who have been off for years and years, discover in a life crisis the need to reconnect.

There is ambiguity in what we know. Not all mainline congregations are losing members, and not all parts of the country are losing to the same degree. Mainline denominations can boast some rapidly growing congregations—the match for almost any specific local growth claimed by any other denomination. In some judicatories growth occurs routinely almost across the board. Statistics get skewed when one judicatory with two large congregations and many small ones reports significant growth—which was limited to those two congregations while sixty others each experienced losses. The truth one experiences locally is more complicated than the statistics.

The fact remains. Membership loss is the overall picture in the mainline denominations. There is no question. Denominational executives and leaders announce membership initiatives, "decades of evangelism," programs with aggressive growth targets. In spite of that, the curves continue downward.

The overall statistics as reported annually in the *Yearbook of Ameri-*

can and Canadian Churches show remarkably consistent curves in
several denominations over the past few decades.[2] For simplicity I will
illustrate with curves for the Episcopal, Lutheran, Presbyterian, United
Methodist, and United Church of Christ denominations.[3]

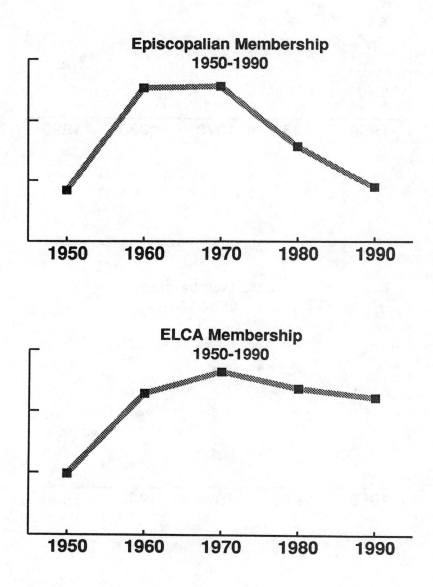

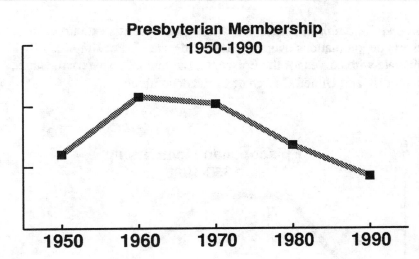

Presbyterian Membership
1950-1990

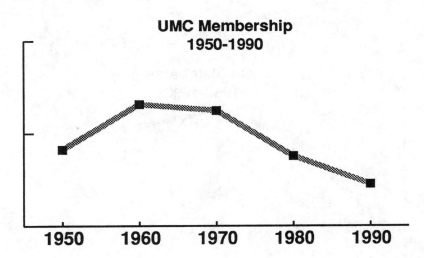

UMC Membership
1950-1990

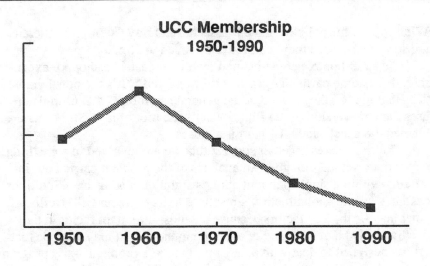

**UCC Membership
1950-1990**

Note that the curves are relatively congruent in shape and direction. They go up and down at similar points along the scale of years.

That is not to say that the denominations have similar numbers of members. The Methodist curve begins at well over nine million members while the United Church of Christ begins at a bit under two million. Methodist can take wry comfort in the fact that they are failing from a higher beginning point than the Presbyterians and Episcopalians. They have a bigger cushion underneath them.

As I have shown these five graphs to people of many denominations around the country, I have sensed their surprise. You see, before seeing all these *different* curves, each group was aware only of its own downward curve. Each had generally thought that it alone had a problem: that it alone had done something wrong. Cause-and-effect thinking had led each to find someone or something to blame to explain the problem they thought nobody else had. Episcopalians blamed a social ministry program called General Convention Special Program (GCSP) of the late sixties. Or the new prayer book. Or the new hymn book. Or the ordination of women. Presbyterians are still blaming the controversy about Angela Davis. Or the move to Louisville. Some Methodists are still blaming Bishop Oxnam or the racism program of the World Council of Churches in the sixties. I imagine UCC members probably still blame Governor

Winthrop for his policies in the Massachusetts Bay Colony! Lutherans are sure it's because they reunited and moved to Higgins Road.

Closer to home, people blamed their own pastor, bishop, or executive, if not some particular practice they disliked. "It's the new hymns!" "It's that motion they passed at the general assembly!" "Our minister uses the new version of the Bible. That's the root of it."[4] Still others blamed the usual catchall—permissiveness.

The five curves together suggest that we are involved in something larger than we had thought. An analysis of the problem carried out internally within a single denomination is simply not adequate. Solutions designed as one denomination's response to its problem will overlook what may be the key factors because the most important factor in the declines may be outside any of the denominations. It may even be that efforts designed to deal with one denomination's problem—any program designed for one denomination—will simply be wasted effort. Something is going on that is bigger than any of the denominations. It is this "something else" that makes me talk about the storm we are all in.

An interesting book from an earlier period—*Understanding Church Growth and Decline*—differentiated between four sets of variables that affect growth curves.[5] It claimed that making sense of the curves themselves requires us to analyze each of four quite different factors: (1) national contextual trends—factors related to the changes in the social and intellectual character of the larger community, the nation; (2) local contextual trends—things going on in the local community and shaping the lives of local residents; (3) national institutional trends—national changes specific to each of the denominational families and often different from those of other denominations; (4) local institutional trends that involve what is happening specific to the congregation one is looking at.

These researchers suggest that growth or decline curves need to take account of all four variables. They argue against too simple or too quick a judgment about where "the trouble" may be.

Church leaders have had all this information before them for at least a decade now. In the nineties articles in *Time, Newsweek*, and many local newspapers have made American laypeople aware of the problem. This awakening of the ordinary congregational member has moved the membership issue onto the front burners of conversation and action and put the professional denominational leaders on the defensive.

I am reminded of the similar kind of public outcry early in the sixties following publication of John Robinson's popular paperback *Honest to God* and the subsequent interview in the Sunday Times of London. Ideas that had been bandied about for a generation or two in theological seminaries of England were suddenly dumped into the public arena. The laity was shocked and upset.

Losses of membership have moved out of the private preserve of the researchers and the church's program professionals and suddenly become public property. And the public—church members—is concerned. Clergy and denominational leaders, particularly among the mainline denominations, are on the defensive.

What can be said about these curves of increasing and declining membership?

Right after the Second World War the mainline denominations experienced a remarkable growth of membership, almost across the board, and that increase peaked by the early sixties. Since about 1965 there has been a strong and continuous decline in membership in mainline denominations; some have lost from 20 to 40 percent of their members.

That is not the whole story. Statistics can mislead, and these curves do. They present a picture significantly more optimistic than facts warrant. They measure the sheer number of members on the rolls of these denominations, not the relationship of the number of members to the number of potential members. Three researchers raise this question in their interesting book *Vanishing Boundaries: The Religion of Mainline Baby Boomers.*[6] It is misleading to look at the sheer number of members without comparing them to general population statistics. It is as if an automobile company were to tell its stockholders how many of its cars were currently on the road without telling how many were sold in relationship to the number of potential buyers out there in the market.

In *Vanishing Boundaries* Hoge, Johnson, and Luidens raise the additional questions of what is happening in the social environment in which the churches exist.[7] That information is even more unsettling for people in mainline churches than the raw membership charts.

Again, the graphs I included earlier in the chapter point to rapid growth of the mainline churches after the Second World War, followed by a period of rapid losses. No one likes to see reduced numbers and strength. That would be true even if the population remained stable. If the membership losses occurred at a period of rapid general population growth, the losses would be much more serious. And that is what happened.

But as far as I know, no one until Hoge, Johnson, and Luidens ever talked about it. Once the *Vanishing Boundaries* manuscript became available, other researchers have made the same point.[8]

In the years charted above, the number of potential members of churches did not remain stable. Actually it increased significantly. The actual population of the country grew by considerably more than a third in those years. Had the denominational membership curves increased by a third they would have been holding their own. The downward curve speaks for itself. But their actual losses when compared to the potential in the population are at least 30 percent worse than the graphs. The graphs we have, disturbing as they are, are misleading and significantly more optimistic than the facts warrant.

Let me put it baldly. What appeared to be a clear decline in numbers begins to look more like a nosedive. There is the curve that describes the population of the United States between 1950 and 1990:

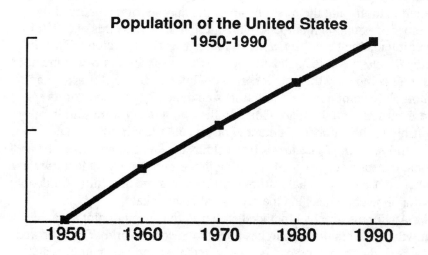

**Population of the United States
1950-1990**

For a period—roughly 1945-1965—the Episcopalians and Presbyterians experienced a significant period of unusual growth, growth without precedent for them. Although all the denominations I cite experienced solid growth in the years following World War II and the baby boom, the growth of the Episcopal and Presbyterian churches outstripped the population growth for a few years. For a while those denominations experienced comparatively more members—and consequently more money—than previously. (Later I will comment on many consequences of this period of unusual growth.)[9]

Episcopalian Membership as a Percentage of the Population 1950-1990

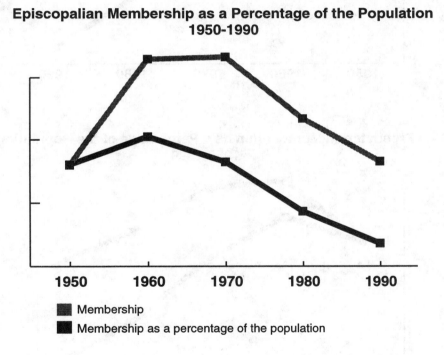

| 1950 | 1960 | 1970 | 1980 | 1990 |

■ Membership
■ Membership as a percentage of the population

(Please note that the figures on which these graphs are based can be located in Appendix B, page 128.)

**ELCA Membership as a Percentage of the Population
1950-1990**

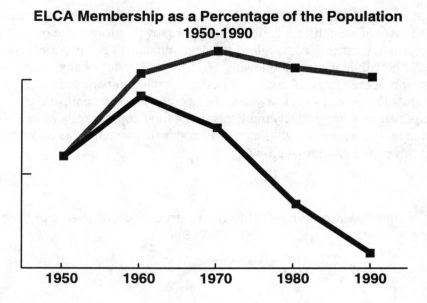

**Presbyterian Membership as a Percentage of the Population
1950-1990**

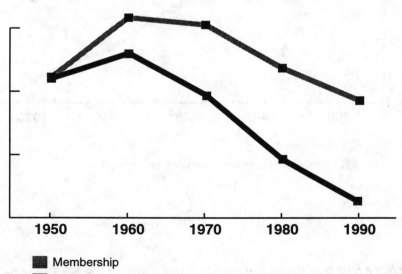

Membership
Membership as a percentage of the population

UMC Membership as a Percentage of the Population 1950-1990

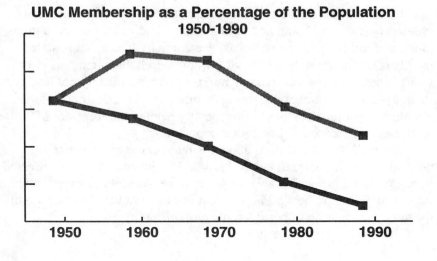

UCC Membership as a Percentage of the Population 1950-1990

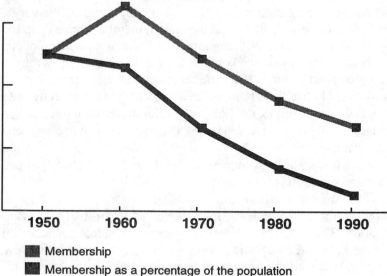

■ Membership

■ Membership as a percentage of the population

The postwar increase of the general population had two main in-
gredients—the baby boom and immigration. And neither of these gives
much comfort to mainline churches. Research indicates that postwar
members of mainline churches had fewer children than members in previous generations, and the congregations are not adequately holding even
those diminished numbers of young members.[10] It is also true that the
mainline denominations have not generally been in the forefront of effective evangelization of immigrant populations.

When all is said and done about the numbers game, the mainline
denominations face significant bad news. I believe the news as reflected
in market share is considerably worse than we have let ourselves believe.
As one looks at numbers of members, it is clear that the churches are in
the middle of a storm of considerable proportions.

That's not all the bad news.

The Money Game

In the area of financing religious institutions, the picture is mixed but
overall no more encouraging than the membership trends. One very
positive piece of news is that mainline church members have risen to
new levels of generosity. Although there has been a significant decline
in membership, the loyal members left are more and more generous to
their religious institutions. Per-member giving has risen more rapidly
than inflation. In the short term, more dollars are being given by fewer
members. As an example, the Episcopal Church, which moved to support tithing at all policy levels, has had a strong response to a concerted
national effort.

But in the long term, resources are likely to decline sharply if present membership trends continue.

I will outline some significant problems.

The members who give are older as well as fewer than in previous
generations. The givers are not being replaced. The full impact of this
will not be known for a decade or two, but it is an ominous bit of news.
The younger generation of members, perhaps caught in the tension of
lower family incomes and higher costs, does not yet seem to have bought
into the level of generosity that marks its elders. Certainly that pressure
is acute where single-parent families are involved. Changes in society

that have required many families to depend on two pay checks have restricted the availability of funding for church programs.

Of course congregational-institutional expenses are rising at least as fast as income. In many locations costs are rising faster than income. The result? A squeeze in congregational budgets for at least the past two decades, a crunch in the budgets of those dependent on congregational offerings (including regional judicatory budgets), and chronic crisis and periodic emergencies in national budgets.

The prognosis for those who depend on congregational financial support is cloudy, to say the least—schools, colleges, seminaries, benevolent agencies. One can understand the aggressive way those institutions are emphasizing planned giving and endowment.

The closer an agency's or institution's ties to the local church, the more likely it is to find support. Denominational leaders tend to see this as reflective of narrow parochialism; I do not agree. The problem simply is that costs are rising more rapidly than income. I see no evidence that it will get better.

Denomination after denomination has engaged in systematic budget cutting every year for twenty years.[11] We do not seem to notice it until there is a cataclysmic shortfall, as has occurred with Lutheran, Presbyterian, and Episcopal churches in the early nineties with major staff layoffs. Looking at the statistics and the trends, I wonder, *Who will be next year's victim?* Remaining denominational staff seem to be saying, with crossed fingers, "Thank heaven it was them and not us. Besides, we fixed the problem when we bottomed out last time."

My statistics do not deal with the emotional toll taken on conscientious staff people in judicatory and denominational offices who face annual cuts in the resources they need to do the jobs they feel called to do and want to do well. Most of the talented staff people I know in national offices have faced year after year of decreasing budgets, with dollar increases less than inflation and with salary increases on hold almost every year. Many of our talented people sit in offices without the funds to mount programs or even call meetings. This has something to do, also, with the adversarial climate that develops between congregations and their regional and national bodies.

A vicious circle exists. Denominational staff people design programs to respond to what they hear congregations needing. They announce the new programs based on what they hope budgets will fund.

Then income shortfalls make no new money available to produce the
programs already announced and expected by congregations. Nobody
takes responsibility for the shortfall. Denominational staff sometimes
mutter about "having to make bricks without straw." We have been
asking them to do exactly that for more than twenty years, and we have
been complaining about the quality of the bricks at least as long. Everybody seems trapped, victimized. The fact is that there is no money and
we do not know how to cut back.

The interrelationship of costs and budgets was dramatically presented to me recently by a Presbyterian friend. "Our experience in 1991
was that national mission giving declined exactly in proportion to the
increase in medical insurance payments for the clergy." As local costs
increase, money is kept "at home," not sent "abroad." When Hartford
Seminary and The Alban Institute collaborated on a study comparing
1970-1980 church statistics in New England and the Middle Atlantic
States to 1970-1980 census data, we found that income to congregations
stayed slightly ahead of inflation for those ten years, but that the congregations' giving to other institutions beyond themselves did not keep up
with inflation (although actual dollar amounts did increase.)[12]

In large, "successful" congregations, it might be easy to overlook the
grass-roots implications of such budget squeezing. But the local import
of this crunch is described by Rev. Gay Jennings in an unpublished report based on her work in the Episcopal Diocese of Ohio. In this report
she has a narrow focus, the economic viability of the "standard" model
parish structure that so many congregations struggle to support.

It is no longer possible to assume that a significant majority
of congregations have the resources to employ a full-time seminary
trained priest as well as support building facilities, program, and
outside giving. Chuck Wilson and Wes Frensdorff published a
study concluding that the budget threshold for this full complement
is between $75,000 and $85,000. In 1992, the Diocese of Ohio has
concluded that the bare minimum needed is approximately $80,000.
That's the magic number. Forty percent of the one hundred and
eleven congregations in the Diocese of Ohio have budgets of less
than $80,000. Almost half our congregations are near, at, or below
the level of financial viability.[13]

She goes on to put her experience in perspective:

> In 1982, only seven Ohio congregations were served by clergy on a part-time basis. Today (1992) thirty-three of our congregations, or just about thirty percent, are served either by cluster clergy or bi-vocational clergy. The Diocese of Ohio is not an unusual diocese. We are not a blip on the curve. And we are not a poor diocese either.

What this talented staff person is saying is echoed across the country in difficult local decisions as conditions change, making it impossible for religious institutions to carry the financial responsibilities they have in the past. Let me be clear—I am not upset that we are being forced to face difficult decisions and make changes. At this point I am simply noting that the financial squeeze is having impact in community after community, denomination after denomination, year after year. It is a part of the big picture, and the news is not good. This is all part of the storm we are in.

The Secular-Society Game

I have already mentioned the Hoge-Johnson-Luidens research, published as *Vanishing Boundaries*. This empirical study of six hundred Presbyterians raises large questions for those of us who would position the churches as a resource to the coming century. I will summarize some of their work.

Between 1989 and 1991 these researchers located about 500 upper-age baby boomers (people who were just under forty-two at the time of the research) and, for comparison, 125 people from a slightly older group. All were Presbyterians, and all had gone through the Presbyterian system as young people up to and including being confirmed. With a lot of persistence and help from local congregations, the researchers contacted most of those on the target lists for telephone interviews.

The full results of these fascinating conversations can be found in their book. For our purposes it is useful to note that as middle-age adults 52 percent of the 625 were still actively involved in church life; 48

percent were in categories defined as "unchurched," but only 8 percent of the total were defined as "nonreligious."

What had led to people "dropping out" of church life?

Clear, definitive answers did not come out. But researchers made some conclusions contrary to the common wisdom espoused in denominational debates.

First, it is not true that many mainline kids have moved to conservative or fundamentalist churches. At least this is not true of the sample we studied.

Second, it is not true that these young people have left because they were sore at denominational leaders or policies. In reality, few know about these matters and few care. The majority aren't interested in denominational politics or even denominational identity.

Third, it is not true that they have left due to attitudes about congregational church life (as opposed to belief factors).[14]

Most of these drop-outs did not drop out primarily because of something the religious institution was doing or was not doing. Rather, it is simply as if the church somehow slipped off their radar screens. It ceased to be important to them.

The researchers hypothesize that the most important factor in the drop-out is not something the churches are doing or not doing; it is the character of the culture surrounding the congregations.

This information is startling and dismaying to church leaders. It suggests that the things we know how to do best have little to do with who stays or who goes. We know how to develop programs. Apparently this population is not interested in programs. It suggests that the very way we organize ourselves to respond to the problem of church dropouts may have very little impact on the people who drop out.

The cultural environment may be more determinative to membership losses than the character of what the congregation is and does. That seems to be the lesson of this particular piece of research. It helps us get perspective on the fact that 80 percent of the people in Alabama belong to a church while only 15 to 20 percent of the population does so in California and Oregon. I have a hard time, much as I love my friends in

Alabama, believing that they are four or five times "better" than my card-carrying church friends in California. What's *outside* the congregation may be more determinative of continuing membership than what's *inside*. Can this also be true of the attraction of new members? Might it also be shaped more by the environment than by what we do inside the churches?

But if the issue of losing members is so greatly a matter of the social environment, how, then, do we address it?

I am not convinced that the researchers have the final word on this one. Is there more we need to know? Yet their research raises the stakes for us in religious institutions. Our very ways of doing anything about the declines may be in question. What do we always do to fix something that has gone wrong? Analyze it and develop a program to fix it.

What happens if the problem does not respond to program? That is the provocative question raised by this research.

In the area of membership losses, we are not dealing with something that is responsive to a new program—even a very good program. We are engaged in a basic interaction between religious institutions and the nature of our social environment. The researchers have lifted the problem to a new level of difficulty and called us to move beyond our narrow answers to address larger issues than we have heretofore had the guts to face.

If I am right, we do not need a new set of programs. We need churches with a new consciousness of themselves and their task. The structures we have inherited have shown little capacity for such radical rethinking of their identity.

That is more bad news for the religious structures we now have. That is another part of the storm we face.

Some Unexploded Bombs That Are Lying Around

I want to describe a few things that I see lying around the churches or the society with the potential for having enormous impact in the years ahead. My vision is narrow: I am thinking about them in terms of how they may well affect our religious structures. It may actually be good for some of these bombs to go off; the society and the churches might fare

better than we are right now. But if any of them were to go off, we
would have to make major adjustments in our thinking.

Tax Policy

Religious institutions are supported by many elements of our govern-
mental tax policies. A few obvious examples:

— When filing income taxes, people itemizing deductions can claim 100
  percent of their gifts to churches.

— The IRS allows people some deductions for property or services that
  a church would otherwise have to pay for. (When I bake twelve
  loaves of bread for my parish bazaar every year, I can deduct the
  cost of the flour from my taxes.)

— Most real estate owned by religious congregations is exempt from
  local property taxes.

— Over and above their salaries, many pastors receive tax-exempt
  income as housing allowances and utility payments.

The case can be and is made that religious institutions provide important,
valuable services to the community. But that case can be made only in a
society that generally looks with favor on religious institutions. My
parents, for example, had no difficulty justifying their paying a little
higher property tax each year to make it possible for the churches in our
town to have "free" fire and police protection. They believed those
churches were important, even the ones they did not belong to. I am not
sure that point is as obvious today to people paying property-tax rates
that have "gone through the roof." Times have changed.
    In many places these tax-exempt policies are likely to remain intact
for another generation or two. Perhaps more. But then what? Only
thirty or forty years ago I never would have dreamed that neighborhood
organizations would oppose the building of a new church. Today in
many communities Sunday morning parking is a more valued resource
than another religious institution. In metropolitan Washington, D.C.,

where I live, churches have serious problems attempting to expand or relocate. Similarly, as local communities and the federal government find it harder and harder to balance budgets, they are sure to reconsider the tax exemptions of church property. Churches will simply have to pay the costs of police and fire services. This will be especially true as property owners who have nothing to do with churches take a jaundiced view of a group that seems to be getting a "free ride" on the backs of their own higher taxes. This many not happen for years in some places, but I think the pressures are inevitable.

My father, a small-town doctor, never charged a cleric of any faith for professional services. That practice was mirrored by drug stores and department stores and many local merchants. Those practices were a way that society's values quietly subsidized religious activity. How quickly those practices change. They seem quaint just one generation later. The only "pastoral discount" I count on is free parking at two local hospitals when I make pastoral calls wearing my clerical collar. Pastors' families have adapted to changes like this, partly by the rapid increase of two-income families in the manse or rectory.

What would happen in your congregation if the pastor's housing allowance became fully taxable? Many congregations would try to find a way to increase the pastor's income by several thousand dollars to compensate for lost purchasing power. Where the congregation simply did not have the resources to do so, the pastor would face a significant effective decrease of income. That has already happened in relationship to Social Security taxes. When clergy became eligible for Social Security several decades ago, they were declared "self-employed" for Social Security purposes. Congregations with the means to do so often give an "allowance" equal to half the Social Security tax (the amount regularly paid by an employer). In congregations that could not provide this payment, the clergy took a significant hit. Some spouses decided to seek employment. Such choices have economic implications for all congregations and for the support of clergy. When money is short, hard choices have to be made.

What would happen if all church property except the worship space were put on the tax rolls of the town? (This is already happening in some places, with argument only over what constitutes "worship space.") What would happen to a congregation's ability to make mission gifts outside the congregation? What would happen to the ability to pay salary increases?

What would happen if charitable deductions were to be limited to 5 percent of taxable income? Or to a maximum amount—say five thousand dollars—to any one institution? Such a "hit" would require pledgers and tithers to do some hard thinking and planning. Some would not maintain their level of giving if the gifts were taxed. What would that do to our ability to keep up buildings and pay salaries, much less make assessment payments to our denominations? (What will happen even this year to small congregations that have to take on new recording and notification responsibilities to help donors justify gifts of $250 or more reported to the IRS?)

My crystal ball does not tell me that any of these scenarios will happen this year or even in the next decade. But my reading of the society says that these policy changes are likely at some time in a world increasingly divorced from religious roots. If past experience says anything to us, any of these changes could happen very rapidly through legal actions.

In summary, a change in tax policy could have direct and negative impact upon how churches do their work.

Medical Costs

This bomb has already started exploding. Medical costs are escalating out of sight. I previously mentioned the impact these rises seem to be causing in the Presbyterian Church. But the impact is across the board. (This very day, as I write, I have received a letter from the Episcopal diocese that carries my credentials. The letter portends a health cost crisis. Either the benefits will have to be reduced or the premium payments made by the clergy will have to be increased.) Every congregation, every pastor, every judicatory will have a rapidly growing worry about this matter, no matter how it funds its medical insurance. Again, there is little churches can do directly: the problem is societal. If these costs are contained in our lifetime, if national universal health insurance is in place and proves to be workable, the rapid increases may come under control. *May* come under control. Until that happens every congregation will face it every year. Every judicatory will face it every year. Every national pension board will face it every year, and many congregations will have to deal with increases every year at budget time.

Actually, medical expense is just one—currently most obvious—

piece of a larger category of potentially exploding commodity costs that could have similar impact. Does anyone remember 1972, when oil prices doubled and doubled again in a few months? Do you remember the struggle with church budgets that had been honed and finally balanced—and then blown out of the water? In our high-tech age there is potential for other unexpected bombs of cost to explode.

The medical cost bomb is already going off, and it has potential for continuing impact on the churches. There may be others. They are bad news.

Litigation

My generation grew up in a world in which no one would have dreamed of suing the church for anything. We now inhabit a world in which people who fall off the curb in front of the church think about suing. Many pastors wonder if they should carry malpractice insurance. Judicatories are already swamped by unexpected legal costs. The burst of sexual misconduct cases of the late eighties and the nineties is a long overdue call to accounting for professional behavior, but it brings in its wake unexplored thickets of liability and cost. Even such routine things as extending a call to a new pastor may require expensive private investigations of personal behavior. It does not seem that these costs will diminish, and they could skyrocket.

Theological Education and Unemployed Clergy

We have invented an enormously expensive form of professional theological education, the graduates of which are priced out of the financial reach of more and more congregations. We are not alone in this. Other professions (legal and medical, to name but two) have developed similar overcapacity for training. My crystal ball does not tell me what might happen in this realm, but I note it as an important worry for us all. Whenever there is such an excess of capacity for training in comparison with the market for services, there is cause for concern.

It is difficult to articulate the full problem. Many denominations really do not know how many candidates for ordination are in the pipeline and how many clergy are needed. It is clear the full-time pastor assigned to one place is affordable to fewer and fewer congregations. Gay Jennings states that in one decade 26 of 111 congregations in her Episcopal diocese stopped being able to afford a full-time pastor.

The other side of the issue is equally challenging. The churches have developed a large cadre of people who feel a powerful call from God to be pastors; they have made real sacrifices to be trained but for one reason or another they cannot be placed in pastoral leadership. They have been displaced for many reasons. In the Catholic church marriage disqualifies thousands of trained pastoral leaders. Many highly trained women ready and able to move into pastoral leadership in that communion are blocked by the prohibition on their ordination. In Protestant churches many congregations who want a full-time pastor cannot pay a living wage. In still other cases well-trained, able female clergy are not able to placed because congregations are not ready to accept their leadership. Thousands of people are trained and would like full-time pastoral positions but are inhibited for one reason or another.   One wonders at the hidden costs of disappointment and bitterness that churches may be storing up in some of their most caring people.

I know of one study that may throw light on this issue: Gay Jennings, whom I quoted above, did another study to find out what happened to people who were selected out *before seminary training*. She discovered that whatever high potential those leaders had when they applied for ordination was effectively lost to the denomination as a result of being "selected out." A high proportion of those disappointed candidates did not return to their congregations in roles of lay leadership but left with anger and bitterness. Speculating from and going far beyond these findings, I worry what will happen to people who seek ordination, go through the rigorous and expensive training for the necessary years, then find their gifts superfluous to the institution for which they had been prepared to sacrifice so much. It feels to me that such a system of stewardship of leaders is fraught with danger. I would certainly welcome further studies in this area.

If we have developed an expensive institution for training pastors, if fewer and fewer churches can pay for those pastors, and if this experience is a negative for trained and unemployed or under-employed people, we have more bad news about the future of the church.

Conclusion

Bad news is never much fun to the bearer or to the receiver. My hunch is that much of what I've written is not a total surprise to my reader. I do not believe I am exaggerating in saying that we are indeed in the middle of stormy seas. The situation the churches are in is much worse than we have been led to think by leaders whistling in the dark, telling us that the troubles have "bottomed out" or that "we are turning around." As I see it, we will not get out of these complex issues in the simplistic ways we have used before. This is not something we can generate a program to fix. A project to increase church membership will not work. Nor will a new improved stewardship program. This news is bad news precisely because what we have done in the past is no longer sufficient. What we know how to do is not going to still the storm. This is not good news.

And yet, I write this book because of my confidence in the religious community and its dedication to trying to listen to and follow God. I want this book to help us end our shallow optimism that everything will turn out all right. I want this book to help us face God's call to reshape our lives and our institutions in faithfulness to God's call into the future. This is not an optimistic call for us to "fix it." It is a statement that we are, indeed, in the middle of a vast storm, the end of which we shall not see.

CHAPTER 2

The Heart of the Matter:
The Apostolic Task of the Church

Going to the Roots:
The Good News and Its Proclamation by Jesus

If the churches are in the middle of stormy times, facing perhaps unprecedented challenges over the next few generations, it is important that we be clear about what we need our congregations to be. If we are to transform the congregations, we first need to get clear about why we need them and what we need them to be for us. Earlier generations had assumptions about what congregations were. Those assumptions worked for hundreds of years, helping Christian men and women carry out what they understood mission to be in their time. Those assumptions led to the establishment of institutions and structures in addition to congregations, all shaped by the church's concern to build Christendom.[1]

Those assumptions no longer work in our times, leading to increasing trouble in our congregations and in the institutions around them. In addition, the storm we are in has led us into confusion about the way that lies ahead. We often feel lost, and with some desperation we cling to familiar parts of the past. With that lost desperation we sometimes defend our congregations and our other religious institutions.

But for what purpose? That's the important question. For what? The question pushes us to look to the roots of what we need congregations for.

One can visit congregations that seem to exist to preserve eighteenth- and nineteenth- century music. I love music enough to hope somebody takes on that task, but I'm not sure that's what I want congregations for—or that that is what they have to contribute. Do congregations exist so they can preserve genteel social structures? I'm not opposed to that, if some people want to do it, but I'm not sure that's what we need congregations for. Are they to preserve an ethnic heritage from the past? Again, I think that's a good thing, but I'm not sure we need congregations to do that. Do we need them to provide meeting places for Alcoholics Anonymous? Do we need them so every community will have a paid pastoral counselor available to those who cannot pay for a therapist? Do we need them to provide a meeting place for people concerned for community betterment? I have no quarrel with any of those as by-products of congregations, but none of them seems big enough, frankly. None of them carries—by itself—the kind of power that comes from connecting with God's purposes and intentions. They are nice enough in themselves, but they hardly provide the kind of energy that turns societies upside down.

What are congregations for? I want to address that issue first. That is what I mean by going to the roots. Once we do that, we can work on how to make congregations move toward fulfilling their purposes.

If the bad news that surrounds us is as pervasive as I suggest, it is all the more imperative that the efforts we make to shape the future focus on the essentials. For me, going back to the roots is to go back to the story that remains normative for me—the biblical record and, within that, the story of Jesus.

The heart of the matter begins in a gospel story in which Jesus goes to his own roots of meaning. He quotes from the Hebrew scriptures, a primary source of his own spiritual nurture, as they are of ours.

Luke's setting is familiar. Jesus has returned to his home town after a series of events that might now be called a vocational crisis. Whatever he had been and known before (and the record is thin) probably after a period in a desert community, this young man, Jesus of Nazareth, has had a life-changing encounter with a prophet at the River Jordan. The impact of his encounter with John the Baptist sent him to a prayerful solitude in the hills–to grapple with God's will for him. What actually took place there in the hills, we will never know; the recorded story of his choices and options is a series of poetic images that probably go back to second- or third-hand interpretations of stories he told some of his friends, perhaps at night by a campfire. From what we later learn of the young man, we can be assured that when he went up to the hills to sort out his life, he did what he did at other moments of crisis: He reflected on the law and the prophets, on the great writings that he knew by heart. He thought and rethought the story of his people in their love-hate relationship with God. He probably hummed the tunes of the psalms or ran through them in his head the way we do with favorite hymns or songs. He prayed. He wrestled with the message of John the Baptist. As he struggled with who he was and was called to be, it is clear that he returned again and again to the words of Isaiah, particularly to what our biblical scholars call Second Isaiah.

When he subsequently went home to Nazareth, home to his family and friends, to his home synagogue, those words of Isaiah haunted him. He chose the text to read as the welcomed home guest:

> The Spirit of the Lord is upon me because he has anointed me;
>> he has sent me to announce good news to the poor,
>> to proclaim release for prisoners and recovery of sight for the
>>> blind;
>> to let the broken victims go free,
>> to proclaim the year of the Lord's favour. (Luke 4:18)

The impact was dramatic. In the context, his friends and family and neighbors recognized a proclamation of identity. *This, my friends and neighbors, is what I am all about.* Although they laughed him out of town for his presumption, we know he spoke the truth because the rest of his life testified to this claim. Here in Nazareth he "talked the talk." For the rest of his life he walked this very walk. When he left the synagogue that day, he started fulfilling his mission, and he did not stop until he was stopped on Golgotha. What did he do? He announced good news; he acted out good news; he demonstrated good news. The good news of liberation. He showed that God's rule was a present reality within the world, that it had the power to overcome all the bad news of the world, all the bad news of illness, rejection, sin, and oppression. This is what he demonstrated the rest of his life.

When we someday sort ourselves out—we who follow this man, we who follow the tradition of this people, we who look to the same Lord who spoke to Abraham and Sarah—I think we will discover that this is what we are called to be about. This vocation Jesus claimed in Nazareth points to the vocation to which we are called, the vocation into which our congregations are called to discover their own identity. His identity led him to identify with and speak to the pain of his world. He invites his followers to that same vocation of demonstrating and proclaiming good news.

If we, too, are to have a role in its proclamation, it is critical for us to get a good fix on what he meant by good news, and how he seems to have interpreted Isaiah's message.

We are not called to copy the specifics of what he did in first-century Palestine; we cannot re-create those conditions.[2] But the stories about what he did and how he tried to communicate his liberating message of good news should give us clues for our own lives. With this in mind, let us look at three short gospel stories that tell us how he did it. Let's consider the stories as if they might be recorded by different ones in our community. I'll paraphrase the first story as might a more liberal theological colleague.

Paraphrase of Luke 4:31-37:
Jesus Heals a Demon-Possessed Man

Once upon a time Jesus was called on to speak at the congregation in Capernaum, a city in his home territory, through which his reputation had spread. The congregants were astonished with the power of his teaching because he minced no words and stated clearly what the scriptures meant. There was no "as Rabbi So-and-So says....and on the other hand, Rabbi This-and-That, speaking for the Jerusalem consensus, puts it this way...." He did not hem and haw, but he spoke clearly and authoritatively.

Well, there was a well-known troublemaker in the congregation, contentious, bitter, constantly disrupting the community and injecting poison into whatever he was part of. He showed up and began to pull his old tricks. Pretty soon the whole congregation was in an uproar. He interrupted, made personal attacks, questioned each speaker's motives, and was generally disruptive.

Jesus spoke directly to him. "Stop. Be quiet. I command you!" The man was so astonished that he fell silent. He was speechless. No one had ever spoken so directly to him or called him to account for his behavior. He sat down. That very evening he began to reexamine his life. Years later both he and others remembered that moment as a crucial turning point in his life.

If you wish, you may take offense at this almost classically liberal interpretation. Take comfort. I almost went so far as to suggest that Jesus convinced the man to go to a twelve-step program! I am well aware that this is not the only interpretation possible, and I use other modes with some of the other stories. This telling suggests something of what may have happened in that synagogue in Capernaum. Perhaps it was much more dramatic, perhaps not.

The point about Jesus' encounter with this demon-possessed man is clear, no matter how we interpret the actions. Jesus directly addressed that man's pain, his peculiar issues or demons. This was no matter of mass psychology. He spoke no generalities. If Jesus' task was to bring good tidings, as he had announced in Nazareth, then it was good news highly specific to this man's bad news. This man was in trouble, and Jesus spoke directly to the trouble. Were there actual demons living in that man? If there were, Jesus spoke to them and took power over them. Is my pale liberal version more palatable to our age than the traditional translations? The record indicates that Jesus dealt with whatever the pathology was. The man's life was transformed at the point of his pain. Jesus recognized and addressed whatever was destroying this man's life. The result? The man was liberated from the demon-possessed life he had previously suffered.

This story is a model of how Jesus acted in situation after situation. He looked to the specific pain in front of him, and he responded to that pain with good news related to the pain. That is the essence of his ministry and the heart of the task of congregations and of everyone who would follow him.

Let us look at another story.

Paraphrase of Mark 8:1-9: The Hungry People

As Jesus' reputation spread, large crowds gathered wherever he was expected to teach. One day an enormous crowd—about four thousand—showed up in the countryside. They were still around three days later, and Jesus was concerned that they might not make it home without some sustenance. When his friends asked what in the world he could do about it, he asked what resources they could lay hands on. When they said they had seven loaves and a few fish, he took what they had, blessed the food, broke it, and fed the people. To everyone's astonishment, there was plenty. As a matter of fact, when they collected the fragments left over, they filled seven baskets—after four thousand people had eaten. Then he sent them all home, full.

This story is told in a more conventional style. But in its own way it makes the same point as the former. Jesus paid attention to the specific character of what was in front of him, and he responded. He had good tidings to proclaim, and he did that for three days. But at the end he became aware of an area of need that he had not addressed: physical need for food so people would not get sick on the way home. Prosaic? Yes, but very real to anyone who was hungry and headed home after three days at a "conference." Jesus tuned in to the specific need—the bad news experienced by that particular group, and he responded to it.

Those of us who live in sacramental religious cultures can richly embellish the story–images of eucharistic worship, phrases such as *bread of life*, meanings of the mystic number seven. But for the purpose of trying to figure out what it means to be a messenger of good news, it is enough to note that Jesus had no difficulty understanding "good news" as serving up bread and fish to hungry people. What seems to matter is identifying a specific need—and responding to it. When he brought good news, it seemed to have direct relationship to pain or to bad news. The people were hungry and he got bread for them.

Let's look at another story, this one from John's gospel.

Paraphrase of John 2:1-11: The Marriage Wine

Early in Jesus' ministry he and his disciples were invited to a wedding, probably of a friend of his mother's because she felt some responsibility for how the reception went. It was a festive occasion, and the guests rather outdid themselves with the refreshments. Jesus' mother noticed that the wine was giving out, and she took her concern to her son. Jesus seemed at first reluctant to respond in such a setting, perhaps thinking, as I am sure I would, that this is a relatively trivial matter, hardly worth getting hot and bothered about. But the mother knew the son and told the servants to do whatever he

asked. Seeing the enormous pots standing there for ritual purification, Jesus told the servants to fill them with water. They did.
Bucket after bucket they poured until all six were full. Then Jesus
told them to serve the water to the guests. Incredibly, the water
turned out to be wine—the finest kind of wine. So fine, indeed, that
the guests commented on it to the host. I'm sure Jesus' mother was
not surprised.

As a story, this doesn't have high drama. There is nothing of life or
death at stake here. What is the worst that could have happened? Some
embarrassment over a shortage of wine? A dressing-down of the wine-
steward for underestimating the heat of the day or the number of bottles
needed for the crowd? In the scale of things, this is no big deal. Jesus
helped some people have a more enjoyable wedding. Yes, there are
other meanings. There is the affirmation of marriage. There are hints of
the eucharistic wine and foreshadowing of Jesus' death. There may be
ambiguity, also. Is the line about changing the ritual purification water
into wine another of the church's anti-Semitic put-downs of Jewish faith
and community? (Somehow we should have learned by now that it is not
necessary to put others down to affirm what one is!)

For our point—trying to understand the task to which religious congregations are called by this wandering rabbi—once again the meaning is
clear: Jesus responded to the need of the people around him. He did not
write out a great check. He did not get another musical group. He did
not organize games for the guests. He did not preach. They were short
of wine; he provided wine. He gave them good tidings—wine. No big
deal.

Three stories. There are many others like them throughout the
gospels. Every one I can think of underlines what I am pulling out of
these three. Jesus always made good tidings available in terms of three
characteristics.

1. For Jesus, good news was always in dialogue with bad news.
Good news is profoundly contextual. For a blind man, good news is
sight. For a lame person, good news is the ability to leap and dance or
even walk. For the guilt-ridden, good news is being forgiven. For the
person in prison, good news is getting out of prison. For the lonely, good
news is community. For the person—or society--crushed by oppression,
good news is freedom. For a person possessed by demons, good news is

to be released from their power. For hungry travelers, good news is food
before they face the journey home. For a marriage running short of
wine, good news is a few buckets of good wine.

2. Therefore, good news comes in many forms. It is not one thing or
one way of doing things or one concept, even. Good news comes in as
many packages as does bad news.

3. These stories lead me to think about Jesus' respect for boundaries.
Each person is allowed freedom. The demon-possessed comes to Jesus
and begs to have his torment ended. The hungry look up to be fed. The
mother asks Jesus for help. Jesus' interventions are not coercive but
responsive. He responds to openness; he does not come with his bag of
tricks to do his thing in spite of those around him. In one case, he even
checks with a lame man before trying to heal him. "Do you *want* to get
well?" he asks. He listens, and where people will open up their bad
news, his good news is ready. He does not force or push his good news,
but he never holds it back.

These are important clues for the purpose of our congregations if we
would try to build congregations that generate good news for our world:
communities that live good news, that turn out bearers of good news;
congregations that are good news to be part of; communities that are
deeply responsive to all kinds of needs, that are able to recognize the
infinite kinds of hurt and pain that we are called to address; communities
that respect and honor the personal and group boundaries by which we
secure our identities. Our congregations are called to be communities
that follow Jesus in bringing good news to the pain of the world.

No small task.

Let me be clear that I know I am walking on slippery ground. These
words and phrases—*good tidings, good news*, and even *gospel*—have all
been translated into the word *evangelism* from the Greek *eu angelion*.
Good news. What I am talking about here is a far cry from what denominations and churches talk about as evangelism. Indeed, I find much of
what churches do in that name singularly wrong-headed and misleading.
The biblical concept to which I am trying to be true is a word of reaching
out, not of gathering in.

I may be arguing for a reinvention of evangelism. I *am* arguing that
this business of communicating good tidings is at the heart of what our
congregations must be about, and it is what our congregations need to be
helping each one of us do.

Let us explore how we might better rethink this central task of every congregation.

Proclaiming Good News in Our Time

Two Models

Growing up as a Christian in the South, I experienced a world that thought of itself as Christendom, even though its actual life was far, far less than that. But in that world I was exposed to two giants of faith.

Although most people around me had an aversion to at least one of the two, from my earliest exposure to them I understood that both were evangelists and both were giants. I met only one of them, and he is now dead. Although I see the other on television occasionally, we have never met. Both were southerners and Protestants like me, so I felt regional kinship with them. One was black; the other is white. Both were Baptists, the predominant faith of the world I knew, far distant from my own low-church Episcopal traditions.

Over the years I watched them, learned from them, and admired them, but I kept wondering how they could be so different, have such different messages, and yet still represent to me what evangelism was all about.

Martin Luther King, Jr., represented the prophetic strand of our heritage, standing strong against oppression. Many people in the white culture in which I grew up, people I cared about, thought he was the tool of the devil. Others thought the sun rose and fell on him. As a child of my culture, I started out with the former group and had to do some growing to discover that he was a true prophet for me. One of the treasures of my life is the worn copy of the *Letter from the Birmingham Jail* I found in my father's effects after his death. I did not know what my father thought of Martin Luther King, Jr., until I found that letter filled with my father's appreciative marginal notes.

Billy Graham is the other giant. The people with whom I normally consort—generally leaning liberal in politics and theology—have such low regard for him that I rarely bring up his name in their company. With those folks I keep Billy Graham as my private closet saint! Early in his ministry I sometimes wondered about his seeming blindness to the prophetic dimensions of faith, but I was willing to leave it to God to sort out the flaws of either of my giants.

I simply knew that personal friends and acquaintances had heard and had their lives changed by the good news one or the other of these two men had spoken. I saw evidence that they had brought good news to situations in which I had previously seen the bad news. That fit my understanding of evangelism. Their words and actions carried the presence of God's kingdom into some lives and situations with which I had personal knowledge.

For years I accepted the fact that my admiration of the two defied rationality; what they were was more important than whether or not they fit into my categories. Struggling with their different gifts as evangelists, however, led me beyond traditional ways of thinking.

If both of them were evangelists, if both of them were bearers of good tidings, then our definitions are simply inadequate. Evangelists are not just one thing and always the same. The truth is more complex than is comfortable. My first clue came when I recognized that King and Graham were speaking from the same gospel, but that each had a different target. They saw the bad news differently. Jesus saw good news as contextual, and that good news differed in relationship to the bad news being experienced at any time. What I was facing was two people, each of whom was committed to the gospel, but each of whom saw a different kind of bad news.

Billy Graham speaks to the bad news he sees as he looks at the human condition. He sees that human beings turn away from God, separate themselves by their actions or their values, and build barriers against God's presence in their lives. He sees such self-centered life as leading to separation from one another and from God; indeed it leads to moral and spiritual death. Although Graham has a place for the community of faith in his message, it is not central because he sees the bad news as so focused in the individual's choice of turning from God. The issues of life and death involve a profoundly individualistic encounter between each person and the grace of God in Jesus. Graham understands that the sicknesses of society come from the profound separation that begins as one woman or one man turns against the grain of the universe, choosing to turn away from God's ever-ready love.

That is the bad news that Billy Graham addresses with his good news. He proclaims that human beings do not have to be condemned to separation and death. He speaks the message that Christ through his cross and resurrection has broken down the walls of separation, making possible true community with one's fellows and with God. All one must do is place trust in Christ. Graham witnesses to the God-given power to turn from the death of self-centeredness to real life centered in God.

If you live with that bad news, if that way of living burdens your heart and life, Billy Graham articulates incredibly good news for you. People I know and love have had their lives transformed by this message. If that is not where you are, the message will likely leave you cold.

Martin Luther King, Jr., knew and preached that same doctrine in most of his sermons to his congregations in Montgomery and Atlanta, but that is not the message for which he is best known, nor was it the good news that made me know him as an evangelist. King saw a very different dimension of bad news. He saw corporate systems whereby one group takes oppressive power over another, destroying the humanity of both the oppressor and the oppressed. He spoke in the context of the issues between the black and white people of the nation, but he saw the larger issues of class and power and wealth as equally oppressive. He saw more than one form of slavery, and he recognized all of them as bad news. He saw the spiritual power of our corporate demons--nationalism, racism, classism—and he saw the pain they brought, binding up Americans and Vietnamese, blacks and whites, rich and poor.

To that specific bad news King preached good news that was quite different from that preached by Graham. He saw and proclaimed that God's love means liberation not only of the soul, but also of human society. King demonstrated that both the oppressed and the oppressor can enter into liberation, and that indeed one party cannot be freed without the other. He saw this liberation as dependent upon the power of God's love. He helped us see that through love the power of nonviolence could overcome the bad news of fear, hate, oppression, and violence within the structures of society.

For those suffering from oppression and social discrimination, and for those who oppress and discriminate, Martin Luther King, Jr., spoke good news. His vision of the bad news and his articulation of the gospel has transformed many lives and has changed the shape of history.

Again, King's way of stating the good news is very different from Graham's, yet both are grounded in the story of Jesus. They speak different messages out of the same gospel because they address different situations. The difference is in how they see the bad news.

So the good news is not some monumental single unity. In this illustration of Billy Graham and Martin Luther King, Jr., we see a continuum of bad news. At one end is the lone individual, lost in self-centeredness and separated from God. At the other end is the social system that destroys through oppression and enforced subjugation.

But I suggest more. A call is involved. Graham and King are drawn to their bad news "targets" by their inner visions and are pulled, almost as if by gravitational pull, toward particular bad news. There is a sense of inner call to match the observed pain with the message perceived in the Jesus story.

This is how I graph two versions of the continuum:

**The Pain
of Individual** ----------------------------- **Corporate
Oppression;
"Society's
Separation
from God**   **Sins"**

**Graham's
Vision of** ----------------------------- **King's
Vision of
Good News**   **Good News**

On this continuum, Graham's vision tends to focus on the left. King's vision tends to the right. Neither man can be captured by a single "location," yet it makes sense to talk about each having a characteristic focus.

I see each of us as having a role as a responder to God's world and the bad news that floods across its face. At this point in your life, where would you place yourself on this continuum? We see and respond to different types of pain. One of us is concerned about the welfare system; another wants to help a particular man at the subway stop. It is not that what others see is less or more important, but just that we see some hurts and not others. Some things grab us; others do not.

I suggest we each may have a giftedness in what we perceive the critical bad news to be. We are drawn to grapple with it, worry about it, and seek to understand the good news that specifically addresses it. Why the attraction? I have no idea. Perhaps our own experience of life or of the power of God opens us up to that particular dimension more than to any other. Perhaps our own weakness focuses our eyes and attention upon one dimension of the good news that most gives life to us. Perhaps we discovered good news as we lived through catastrophic bad news and were forever sensitized to that pain.

A basic theme of this book is that the ability to "see" bad news relates to our discipleship. The willingness to "do something" about it relates to our apostleship.

I suggest that the inner pull to respond is much more than a pull or an attention grabber. It is no less than our perception of *call*. It is our open door to the good news we have to share. (See the Appendix A for an educational design I use to help people work with these ideas to locate different perceptions of bad news in their lives.)

Jesus' good-news proclamation had three characteristics: It is related to specific bad news; it appeared in contextually appropriate forms; and it was respectful of individuality and personal boundaries.

Is it really a surprise that each of us is called to our own vision of the pain of the world, that each of us has a voice to speak something unique to a special reality of the world?

I believe that this individual sensitivity is a clue to where our call to service may lie. Among all the possible things out there in the world that cause pain and hurt, there are some—perhaps only a few—that claim us, that call us to bring good news. I sometimes say that every pain in the world has a special kind of Velcro on it, and that each of us has grown a patch of our own special brand, also. We can bump into all sorts of pain out there, but we do not respond until there is a match. Then we have no option. We are seized by the pain that matches our call, and we must act.

There is no magic in this understanding of vocation. Nevertheless, I think this pull, this sense of being seized, is God-given and helps us sort out what we will do with our lives, what jobs we try to take, and what causes we sign up for.

Congregations have a stake in this dynamic because their task is to help us become carriers of good news. Training in discipleship involves increasing the sensitivity we have to the pain of the world at the same time that we are more deeply engaged in the good news of the Jesus story lived out in our congregation. More about that later.

A More Wholistic Model of Proclaiming Good News: A Map of Evangelism

Another dimension to this simple continuum broadens our understanding of what it means to be a proclaimer of good tidings.

As I thought about the differences between Billy Graham and Martin Luther King, I realized that the continuum described above identifies only one of several dimensions. It targets the bad news but ignores the framework within which one is called to serve.

Graham understands the response to the bad news of estrangement from God to be articulated and acted out in a "religious" context and with "religious" language. Consequently he speaks of sin and salvation; his calls to action are to make "a decision for Christ"; the movement he urges is into religious community and sustenance.

King, from a very similar religious tradition, came to represent a response in the "secular" context with "secular" language. Where he perceived systems oppressing the human spirit, he called for action mostly in the social arena outside religious institutions. Consequently he spoke language of oppression and freedom; his calls to action were to meet violence with nonviolence on city streets; the movement he urged was within the secular social structures, the judicial systems—the political and economic realms.

This brings me to a very broad map of what is called for if we are to

be a community proclaiming good tidings. Instead of a linear continuum, I see a map that includes great diversity of vocations, not just
one way to proclaim good tidings. I see a map that encompasses a larger
vision for the religious task of congregations than I generally see. Here I
outline that map as a grid that includes a vertical continuum suggesting
the different styles with which one might respond—from a religious style
to a secular style.

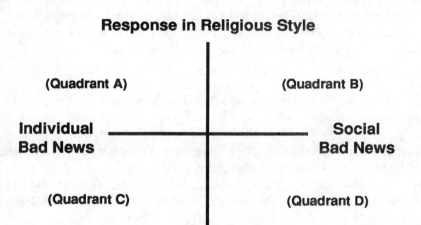

I share this schematic as a pointer to truth, not as truth itself. Like
all schematics, it oversimplifies and exaggerates. But it is a useful tool
to point to the kinds of work I think congregations are called to enhance.
This picture can help us enlarge our vision of the field of evangelism, the
arena in which we are called to be bearers of good news.

Again, can you place yourself on this map? What bad news most
frequently grabs your attention? And how do you usually respond? I am
sure one's point of sensitivity and response changes from time to time.
So location is simply an approximation of where one is right now.

As on the continuum, there is no "bad" place on this grid, nor is one
quadrant "better" than the others. Billy Graham's call to evangelism is

not better than Martin Luther King's. Nor is King's better than Graham's. They are different perceptions, different callings. Indeed, as I pointed out in the case of King's preaching as opposed to his "public" ministry, it is possible for one person to respond in more than one way to the hurts of the world. At different life seasons we may locate ourselves more in one area than another, only to discover ourselves pulled or called to another way at another time. As I have already suggested, King ministered in his congregations in a style one might identify with quadrant A. Within his leadership of the Southern Christian Leadership Conference, his location on the map was more toward quadrant D.

Each of the quadrants points to a different set of sensitivities to vocation and evangelism. Let us look at them briefly, one by one.

Quadrant A. People whose life and faith stories make them particularly sensitive to an individual's needs and who have an internal compass set within religious categories would likely find themselves in quadrant A. Such people, one might speculate, would bring strength to one-on-one teaching and care ministries. They might be at the heart of a congregation's ministry of intercessory prayer, but even more so of contemplative prayer. These people are sensitive to spiritual lostness and yearning and generally unafraid to speak directly from a wellspring of faith-language and faith-experience. Such people would be frustrated and useless in most committees and would flee social projects like the plague. Some might make gifted spiritual directors. I locate much of Billy Graham's ministry in this quadrant.

Quadrant B. These people are aware of how people need each other. They are tireless in supporting the congregation's corporate activities. They tend to support denominational programs and institutions, such as colleges and seminaries, and counseling centers and care programs established by the congregation or denomination. They are generally good members of worship task forces and heavy supporters of study programs—the more biblical the better. Pastors and rabbis in charge of congregations need to "spend some time" in this quadrant, whether or not it is the center of their lives. Much of my own life—some forty years of working in, with, and for congregations—tells me that this is home territory for me, although I have periods in which I have focused elsewhere.

Quadrant C. What I call the anonymous saints dwell in this quadrant. I think of people who go through life doing what needs to be done, some of them in quite humble circumstances and some in prominent roles, but who never say much about it. I know a garbage collector in Washington who runs an evening tutoring program for black junior-high kids. I think Dag Hammarskjold may have belonged here—his life and work as an international statesman undergirded by a remarkable but unspoken spiritual life. I think of my father's life-long ministry as a doctor and community leader who rarely said much about his faith. These may be the people who show up at early morning services but never serve on the board. They are known in the community by how they treat people and make a difference, but they are embarrassed to be asked much about their congregation. Most people they work with may not even know they belong to a congregation.

Quadrant D. These I call secular saints. They see the primary focus of their lives to be service to the hurts of society. Some are articulate with prophetic power, while others are foot-soldiers in one revolution or another. Such people often get irritated at the slow pace of the congregation in being able to "get on with it," and they can be severe critics of the values incorporated in a denominational budget. Their center of gravity is not the congregation or the denomination, but their compulsion to respond to social needs. More than a few of them become religious "alumni," actually leaving religious structures and life to try to change the character of the world without a continuing link to a congregation. I suspect that many who populate environmental associations would find themselves here. Such people often leave the religious community because of the values they learned in that very community; they are unable to "wait" for the congregation or church leaders to respond to the pressing needs they see in the world.

Use your imagination, for a moment. Look at that grid—all quadrants—and you will be looking at the whole realm of bad news. You can differentiate, as we have, among different kinds of bad news and different needs for good news in the lives of people and the structures of society. It is a map of—or a window on—the needs for God's good news, for evangelism. Looking out that window, we see the fields white with harvest—as near as our imagination, as varied as our callings. The variety of needs out there represents our need to send an apostolate as varied as the needs.[3]

In terms of the qualities represented by these quadrants, congregations need to be as comprehensive as possible, not because diversity is a modern fixation, but because the needs we face are across the board. A congregation that lacks people from any one of these quadrants will lack something the ministry needs for its health. A congregation that overbalances itself or its program in one quadrant does so at the cost of missing important areas of need.

I believe the task of congregations is to do two things at once: (1) to help more and more people look through that window to the world to identify what needs call out to them, and (2) to nurture and strengthen each person and send each out to use unique gifts to respond as only he or she can. As members identify their calls and are nurtured and sent, we will see the development of the apostolate of the future church.

Congregations of the future need to be congregations that nurture varieties of sensitivities to the bad news of the world and respond to those many forms of pain. These will be congregations open to more than one point of view.

Every member of the church stands before an imaginary window, facing all the need and hurt of the world. Most, but not all, of us feel a pull to engage with some of that pain, whether it is physical pain or homelessness, ignorance or spitefulness, hunger or illness, guilt, a sense of lostness, hopelessness, or despair.

A congregation's task is to help us to know and claim the power we have, commit ourselves to engage the pain of the world, and then to manage the process by which we are transformed from passive onlookers to sent people—apostles. Our congregations are there to help each of us grasp and be grasped by the good news that God has uniquely for each of us, and then to empower us to go out as sent people—apostles—to the pain of the world as bearers of our own special version of the good news.

The story of Jesus leads us to become disciples and apostles carrying forth the kind of good news that Jesus modeled—a good news that is profoundly contextual, touching the different kinds of pain present at any place; a good news that comes in many shapes and sizes; a good news that always leaves the recipient free to accept or reject it. Congregations, then, are about helping us all become disciples and apostles.

The root of it all is transformation. The transformation of each of us into a disciple whose life has been touched and shaped by Jesus' good news. The transformation of each of us into a special part of the apostolate Jesus is calling into being to proclaim his reign over all.

CHAPTER 3

The Task of the Congregation: Transformation – Preparing Disciples and Apostles

In the last chapter we stood before an imaginary window that looked out over the world, and we speculated about all the needs out there for committed action and caring. That window looks out across the landscape of the world in which the variety of human and social bad news calls for those sent to bring *eu angelion,* good news. That is the field for the action of the apostolate.

Looking out that window onto the world one can see a vast cacophony of hurts and pain, inhumanity and injustice. The ability to see the world's pain as a field for engagement comes only to those impelled by a religious vision. Having such a vision is what it takes to become an apostle. Helping transform ordinary people into apostles involves first helping them discover their discipleship.

In this chapter we will start by reversing the window perspective. Having stood behind the window looking out into the world, now we step outside and look back through the same window. Now we focus on the inner life of the congregation itself. What needs to happen there to support and send apostles into the world? Having looked at the critical functions that build up disciples, we can then address the process by which disciples are transformed to enter the apostolate.

As we looked out the window, our focus was on the apostolate–the work of church members in the world, bearing witness to the kingdom of God and seeking to bring it to reality in the midst of the world's pain. As we turn around and look back through the same window from the world into the congregation, our focus is on those processes that call out discipleship and nurture each person in ever deeper discipleship.

In the New Testament, building on the traditions of the Hebrew scriptures, particularly the prophetic literature, Jesus announced the beginning of a new kind of human community. He called it the kingdom or reign of God. Within that realm he described what Isaiah and Jeremiah dreamed of—a place where the poor were cared for, the sick healed, where the blind received sight and widows were supported. A place where those who were lame could come to leap with joy and where those who were in prison or oppressed would break free of their prisons.[1]

Jesus announced that this kingdom had already begun, and his actions were based on the reality of the kingdom. In his announcement of the new society and in his actions, there was power. The new society began as he acted. The Word led to the actions. More than that, he invited his fellows and followers to act in the power of that kingdom.

They did. I think of the remarkable story in Acts 3. Peter and John, going up to the temple, run into a lame beggar at the Beautiful Gate. The story picks up drama. Their purses are empty, and they have nothing visible with which they can respond to his need. Is the beggar out of luck? No. Peter acts in the power of the new kingdom. He says, "I have no money, but I can give you something else. Get up and walk." You know the story. The lame man got up and walked. I'm convinced that the lame man was stupefied to find himself cured. I think Peter was, too. The good news seized him *as he acted* for the new world. He had the power to engage the demons of the world before he knew he had the power. He was a potential apostle until he acted as an apostle. It was his stepping out to act for healing that made his apostolate real.

Had Peter not acted on the presumption of the kingdom, the lame man would not have walked, the power to cure would not have appeared, and Peter would not have become an apostle. What made Peter act beyond his knowledge? What made him go beyond his previous faith? I have no answers to this set of questions because I think we are on the edge of the relationship between one's faith and that in which one has faith; it is not fully a matter of Peter or of God, but of a life-dialogue between them. We can use pale language—*vocation, faith-response, leap of faith*—but I am not sure we will ever capture the mystery. God offered Peter the option, and Peter took it. The kingdom appeared when Peter acted in its power.

I think the task of the local congregation is to help ordinary people become engaged in that mystery, people willing to make the leap from the known to the unknown as Peter did; people who act on the basis of the new society, who claim the power of that kingdom, who then act for peace and justice and love and healing. The congregation's task is to call that faith forth in us and send us to act with no positive assurance that anything at all will happen.

In all the complexities of history, in all the encounters with organizational realities, in all the theological debates and philosophical analyses, I think we have lost sight of that simple focus of faith. I have no idea if congregations will grow or decline if they act on that focus, and frankly I don't give a damn. But I know they will lose their soul if they don't. That part is simple.

How to do it is not.

I want to make it clear that there is much mystery in what I want to talk about. I will describe established ways by which we have developed disciples and processes of transformation. I will begin a conversation about how we may go further in our congregations. But I confess that I do not have final answers. This may be like reading a dialogue but having a script that includes only one character's lines. There is another actor who speaks and moves in ways we do not control or always understand, but of course that party is key to the dialogue. (In Jesus, my tradition teaches and I believe, the two sides of the dialogue spoke with one voice and acted with one will.)

As we think about this mysterious process of transformation by which people begin to act as citizens of the new society, I want to explore four functions, traditional to congregational life: (1) the community within the larger society—what the early church called *koinonia*; (2) the life-giving processes summarized as proclamation—what the early church called *kerygma*; (3) the lore, the tradition, the stories, and their transmission with power—what the early church called *didache*; (4) the role of serving—what the early church called *diakonia*. Each of these functions is a means for the transformation of ordinary people into disciples and a necessary support for a life of discipleship. The stronger these functions, the more likely the congregation is to be an active apostolate reaching out to the bad news of the world.

Koinonia: The Congregation as Community

The regular oscillation of the church person between the outward life of the public and the inner life of the congregation is the stage for much transformation. Facing outward, congregations open up to a public world in which their members engage, are influenced, and exert influence. Facing inside, congregations are an environment for growth and support. In *koinonia* a member of a congregation lives in the tension of religious heritage and public arena.

The outward engagement of the congregation with the public is a critical issue for today's world. Parker Palmer has opened up for us a vision of what that public world is or should be:

> The word "public" means all the people in a society, without distinction or qualification. A public school is a place where no child is barred from entering, a place where the common culture of a people can be passed along to the next generation. A person in public life is one whose career involves accountability to the people as a whole, one who carries a public trust. Even the weaker phrase, a public figure, means a person whose life is visible to all who care to watch it. When information appears in the public press it is available to everyone, and a public library collects and stores such information so that it will be available to persons yet unborn. And the word is used in less grandiose ways, as in the English "pub" or public house, which is a gathering place for the whole community.[2]

One reads this description with nostalgia because *public* has many negative connotations today. Palmer explores why this rich concept of a deep bond that can bring a diverse people together has degenerated into a term that makes us think of interest groups competing with one another for a place at the "public trough." He suggests that the rich potential of the word *public* has been eroded by our willingness to give away the care and maintenance of our common life to external, impersonal, often political structures. He argues (as do Robert Bellah and his colleagues in *Habits of the Heart*[3]) that the public realm becomes a sea of competitive forces and society becomes a conglomeration of aggressive and defensive organizations and people locked into competition for resources.

With a public vision of life limited by what the law allows, we create a self-fulfilling prophecy. Palmer continues: "fewer and fewer people venture into public without being well-armed (figuratively and literally!) Small wonder that more and more people retreat from the public arena...into the sanctuary of private life." Society and government cannot generate a vision of a "public life of variety and breadth, a life in which the human impulse toward community is drawn out and encouraged." Government can and does help competing groups balance their different interests; it can protect those who cannot protect themselves; it can punish those who offend the public order; but it cannot produce a vision of what it means to live in community. It cannot generate community.

Palmer's insights echo biblical language in Paul's convoluted discussions of law and grace. Society can define itself and set limits, but we all yearn for a community in which we know that we are cared for and valued in ourselves. Society can help us defend our prerogatives, but it cannot help us reach out to others (or others reach out to us.) Society can define what is fair and legal, but it cannot make our hearts care for others, particularly those who are different from ourselves. Law is essential for life together, but it is incomplete in itself. We want and need more than society by itself has to give.

On the most mundane level, public law can define gross misconduct as felonies, but law cannot eliminate the patterns that lead to felonies. It can lock up people who commit felonies, but it cannot produce people who love to do good and who love mercy and care about their neighbors. Some believe the problem of crime in our society can be solved by stiffer sentences and better law enforcement. In this conversation about public life we can say quite clearly that you cannot hire enough police and you cannot build enough jails to produce a public life of meaning and value. That is a dead end. Though perhaps necessary, it will not lead to a vision, a hope, and action for a realm that is governed by self-giving rather than self-aggrandizement.

The larger society *needs* the community graces that are vital to church-congregational *koinonia*. As citizens become disciples within the congregation, they build the potential to be carriers of grace within the public realm. Congregations are laboratories that can prepare us for public living and service. In congregations citizens can be generated as provocateurs of grace within a society shaped by law.

Ten Features Characteristic of a Good Congregation

Palmer lays out ten features that he says are characteristic of public life
—as it should be. How can each open up to us the opportunity to move
creatively back and forth between our two worlds?

These ten characteristics of the public and my reflections on them
suggest the wealth of the gifts that congregations bring to a nation (or a
world) that seeks to become *community*. Indeed these congregational
gifts may be essential to the building of a viable public life. At the same
time, this is no one-way street. A dialogue with these characteristics of
the public world may provide new depth to the life of congregations.

The word *dialogue* is critical in this discussion of *koinonia*. This
calls for engagement.—engagement that brings strength to each world.

In Palmer's public:

1. Strangers meet on common ground. Dare we assume that strangers bring gifts, not threats? In today's outside world we are taught to
steer clear of the stranger. "Don't make eye-contact!" But it hasn't
always been this way. In our congregations we have a laboratory for
reaching out beyond ourselves and our families. Can congregations open
us up to at least civility to those beyond our community of family or
friends? Dare we think of the possibility of a public world ruled by the
values of hospitality? Can our congregations demonstrate that possibility
to each of us personally and train us for that kind of public life? Can
congregations raise up disciples who live apostolically in the public
world?

2. Fear of the stranger is faced and dealt with. We do have fears
about people who are not "like us." We have all sorts of stereotypes and
prejudices, all kinds of unexplored myths about "others." Such paranoia
cripples the social order and sets discriminatory processes in stone. All
congregations, even the most seemingly homogeneous, have within them
a mixture of ages and sexes, points of view and backgrounds. Can our
congregations be seen as safe places where we can reach across boundaries, where we can support experimentation? Indeed, many congregations have a history of sending groups of members into other communities to work and socialize with others—pounding nails, digging ditches, or
stitching layettes. Within the safety of a congregational work-group, the
individual disciple can more easily join the stranger-community in common work. Can our congregations become intentional laboratories for
exposing us to people outside our groups?

3. Scarce resources are shared and abundance is generated. In our society this essential characteristic of public life may be as threatened as any. We seem to be a social order in which the rich get richer and the poor get poorer. Who is there to speak for and act on another vision? Who will speak if not the children of the scriptures, the Book in which poets and prophets made it crystal clear that God has a special concern for the poor among us? In the last decade I do not think I have seen a congregation of any sort, big or small, rich or poor, that does not take a regular offering or other action to get food to people who do not have enough. In our larger cities a very high percentage of hungry people who receive a free meal get that meal at a local congregation. It is so much a part of our life that we don't realize how unusual our actions are. Sharing resources is just what life is "supposed to be." There is no big deal, no brass bands. It is just who we are and who we are trying to become. As we act on our vision, we are saying something to our society about what public life ought to be. We are acting in the power of the new society. In the public realm our social order speaks with fear of diminishing resources: If you get yours, there is less for me. Our biblical heritage speaks of abundance, not scarcity: The more you have, the better I will be. Can we bring this consciousness to the world we inhabit? Can we nurture it in our congregations, or are we, too, going to become locked into scarcity thinking? In the years immediately ahead, as resources are more and more limited in our religious institutional life, as everyone around us in churches and in the public realm is talking of cutting budgets, we may have a more and more difficult time witnessing to abundance as disciples. There will be tests of our discipleship!

4. Conflict occurs and is resolved. Our congregations, whatever else they are, are seething pools of conflict. We have different ways of decorating altars, and we fight about it. We have different ideas about who the pastor should be, and we fight about it. Sometimes our fights are donnybrooks, but more often they are the tight-lipped, controlled, hard-to-finish type. The grudge-generating kind. Some fights turn into feuds that last generations. Sometimes those outside congregations are more comfortable than we in dealing with differences. We "religious" folk have a way of calling God in to the fight to help us destroy the opposition.

But times are changing. We are trying to learn how to reach consensus, how to rebuild when fights fracture our communities. Our tradition

brings perspectives about forgiveness and reconciliation that help us
reach out to one another for community, not just cessation of hostility.
As we deal with our differences, we learn about reaching beyond hostility in the public world toward a different vision of society. Can we learn
to use our own spiritual resources of forgiveness and reconciliation within our own communities, learning to bear witness to the same power in
the world outside our congregations?

   5. Life is given color, texture, drama, a festive air. Every act of
worship should be a laboratory in celebration of community. It is interesting to note that religious communities invented drama and music
and probably public festivals–all pointing to the rich possibilities of
community beyond fear and conflict. These dimensions in our congregations and in our communities give us opportunities to dramatize a one-
ness and commonality with others. A church on Easter, a town park on
the Fourth of July–both speak to what *community* means, and our presence involves us in that community. Congregations need to help their
members engage in celebrations of community and engage the public in
its celebrations that pursue a vision of what the larger community is
called to be.

   6. People are drawn out of themselves. The locked doors and barred
windows of city living, the residential sections protected by armed
guards and attack dogs–these realities speak vividly of the isolation
toward which our society pushes us. Congregations cannot leave this as
the last word: We have a mandate to reach out and to bring in. We bear
a high tradition of hospitality. In that sense congregations are counter-
cultural–or at least counter to the way the culture is drifting. As congregations reach out to the isolated, they become places where the isolated
can engage with others. In a society with strong pressures toward pri-
vacy, the public realm needs congregations to have vision to root people
out of their hidden aloneness and train them for community. Members of
congregations need to become neighborhood leaders helping citizens
enter the lives of their neighbors.

   7. Mutual responsibility becomes evident and mutual aid possible. I
have already noted the matter-of-factness with which congregations assume they are supposed to do something about the hungry. Many congregations have a list of people to pray for—the sick, the shut-ins, the
grieving. And many have cadres deployed weekly to take flowers to the
sick, to take elements of the Eucharist to those who cannot get to church,

to call on people in the hospital. The church I walk by on the way to my office has a whole set of parking places reserved for three hours daily for those who come to take Meals-on-Wheels to shut-ins. Taking responsibility for one another is taken for granted in our congregations but not in our public arenas. In this area can our ordinary community life be a beacon to our society at the same time that it prepares us to offer these gifts of service outside our congregational bounds? And should not congregational members be among those who lead and carry out efforts to rebuild neighborhoods and encourage citizens to care for one another's safety and security?

8. *Opinions become audible and accountable.* In this "characteristic feature of public life" I must admit that congregations have as much or more to gain from as to give to the public. The modest political systems within congregations need to be opened up to the candor with which public figures articulate and defend positions. Congregations would be strengthened by more such accountability. Having said that I also note that congregations and their members do have much to contribute. They generally have a feel for the legitimacy of opposition, for the ultimate value of those who oppose one another. Congregations can bring a dimension of civility to public contention.

9. *Vision is projected and projects are attempted.* People in congregations are regularly exposed to transcendent visions of what life is supposed to be. They seem indefatigable in trying to address hurts and pains they see. If they are to be faulted it is because of the quixotic nature of some of their projects–going up against human evil (or city hall) with water pistols. Yet an invaluable gift congregations bring to public life may be the way their hope is grounded theologically in this conception of God. Congregations bring persistence to the table. Because their visions are grounded in an understanding of God and God's purposes, congregations are not as likely as the general public to drift away from important visions—such as caring for each person. Congregations are grounded in a sense of God's purpose and movement through history— something that does not fade after a few defeats, as does political optimism. There is a big difference between optimism and hope. Congregations bring the latter. In a gun-flooded society, congregations know about a world in which swords are turned into plowshares. In a society of gangs and drugs, congregations witness to a world in which the lamb and the lion can dwell together. We bring visions. That is part of what we are.

10. People are empowered and protected against power. The
checks and balances of governing structures should provide a framework
that protects the citizen against unwarranted assumptions of power. At
the same time, these structures give space and scope for a citizen's gifts
to be shared. Congregations, in their life of worship, act out and celebrate the importance of freely given gifts shaped and conformed by
structures of authority and custom. They also understand the limits of
human integrity, the presence of sinfulness, and the necessity for larger
frames of value.

Koinonia and a Congregation's Critical Distinctive Identity

Congregational community life has always been understood as the locus
of the ordinary church member's growth and development. This is true
despite the fact that for a thousand years or more it has been assumed
that one "picked up" and absorbed *from the society* one's knowledge of
faith and grounding in one's heritage. The whole world of Christendom
—rather than the life of the congregation itself—was the "teacher" of the
faith. It was something that happened without having to pay attention to
it, as one might "pick up" decay-proof teeth by drinking fluoridated
water. That was basically the Christendom assumption. Community
religious festivals, the legal codification of a value system, and the character of life in the society was understood to ground and root one adequately for spiritual growth. During this period the faith-community
suffered a loss—its ability to distinguish itself from its environment. As
the faith-community was swallowed up in the cultural environment, it
lost its sense of "distance" by which it could understand its distinctive
identity and the distinctive nature of what it had to offer to and receive
from the environment. Social scientists describe this as the loss of a
sense of boundary. A community will have little to offer a larger society
if it cannot distinguish itself from that society, and it will not long maintain its distinctive heritage if it cannot train new members in what is
special about the community itself.

If our congregations are to nurture their members, empowering
them to be disciples and apostles, we must take a hard look at a surpris-
ing gap between the experiences ordinary people have of God and the
experience they have of their local congregations. Over the past two

decades a number of researchers have been surprised to discover a very large number of people who have had what they identify as direct experiences with God or transcendence.[4] Of course, there is ambiguity in the reports, but the surprise has been in the widespread nature of the phenomenon.

Several of us discovered—and Jean Haldane later discovered independently—that people do not connect those experiences with the religious congregations to which they belong. Haldane pointed out that ordinary people who have extraordinary spiritual experiences often do not think that their congregations or clergy would be interested in or able to help interpret such experiences. It is as if people have separated deep personal religious experience from congregational life. They feel that the congregation expects their support and attendance at worship and activities, but that the congregation has no interest in their religious experience.

I know that seems absurd. But it is a sign of how much we must do to rethink the character of community within our congregations. Congregations must let go of their preoccupation with programs and activities if they cannot also be a home in which religious experience and religious yearning is welcomed and nurtured. We need congregations with a sense of community in which each person's experience of God is affirmed—or at least brought into the open.

Congregations need to provide space for intimate storytelling that encourages members to share those deep experiences with one another. We need to develop spiritual directors in every congregation–the ministry seen as a matter of course, not only and always as a function of "professionals." We need congregations that take the experience of God as the norm. We need congregations that expect healing to be part of one's faith-life, whether or not one uses the ordinary medical arts. Healing may be as life changing with the help of Blue Cross/Blue Shield as it can be with the help of laying on of hands. Our congregations need to be the places where all of these experiences are seen as related to a life of faith.

Left outside the worshipping community, such experiences can lead to all kinds of psychic pathology. Paul was obviously both drawn to and nervous about such experience in the early church. He wrote appreciatively of the power of speaking in tongues, but he was also eager that such gifts be brought under the discipline of the community. The congregation-community has little chance of influencing such practices toward health if it refuses to pay attention to the lack of this necessary part of *koinonia*.

At this point I simply note a continuing congregational weakness—their inability to identify and communicate to members their distinct nature. This inability handicaps our congregations in fulfilling their purpose and mission to their members and to the outside world.

Koinonia Wrap-Up

Congregational members live in the tension of their two worlds. They move back and forth as citizens of two realms—the public and the religious—potentially enriching each. Within the congregation, they inhabit a community that celebrates and tries to understand God's realm of shalom. Within their own bounds, congregations are communities of growth and support. This makes them a key resource for the transformation of each member. In this area we have much work to do if congregations are to fulfill their function of making disciples. When disciples move into the public realm, as apostles they bear with them the marks of God's realm.

As one looks from the congregation outward to the world, one can see the "good news" of the very presence of the congregation as it relates to and in that larger world. In the midst of a public community that is increasingly divided and antagonistic, where contention is the rule, it is good news to see islands of community that live by a different set of values. Congregations can assist in the transformation of society simply by being places where a different kind of community life is experienced and witnessed to. This ability to incarnate community is far more important as good news in the world than congregational "outreach programs." In this sense, congregations are communities that can be transforming influences in and examples for the world outside.

Congregations remain one of the key places where self-centered citizens may be transformed into disciples ready and eager to become bearers of good news to the needs of the world. And from these places the power of God's community can begin transforming a society into a community.

Koinonia, long a key characteristic of the congregation, remains a key to the congregation's ability to be a transforming reality for members and for society.

Kerygma: The Proclamation of Good News

Congregations have traditionally been the places where as a people we have been grounded in our story and in its meanings. Story came first, literally. Both the Hebrew scriptures and the New Testament existed as stories recited in community long before anything was written down. Congregations gave birth to scriptures. In congregations the storyteller was asked to tell the stories, and those congregations passed the stories along, sometimes bending them a bit in the passing. There is no way to go deeper into our heritage than through the stories faithful people passed on through their congregations to future generations.

The stories have always had transforming power. Nathan told a story to King David, a simple story of a rich man with many flocks and a shepherd with one precious lamb. When Nathan described how the rich man took the shepherd's one ewe lamb, David was outraged at the character's aggression. When Nathan, referring to David's sin against Uriah and God, said, "Thou art the man," David heard. The story carried power to convict and to transform.

Jesus told stories that have been retold generation after generation, and the stories have new power in each generation. The story of the Good Samaritan has spoken to prisoners of war and their captors. It spoke to Florence Nightingale. It spoke to me as a young man about racial injustice. In these days, it speaks to men and women who bear responsibility for policy about ethnic strife in the former Yugoslavia. That simple story leads to sleepless nights for policy makers two thousand years after Jesus told it to his followers. I will have more to say about story below, but first I turn to a special way in which congregations have come to encounter the transforming power of stories.

Churches speak of the power of the Word to transform life. They understand "the power of the Word" to mean scripture, yes, but also profound reflection upon it. They have experienced its transformative power in the act of preaching. In response to that strange, familiar activity of preaching, for generation after generation, gathered congregations have been transformed by the spoken word.

Who knows what all happens in preaching? Phillips Brooks, perhaps the best Episcopal preacher[6] since John Donne, spoke of it as "truth communicated through personality." William Dols, executive director of the Education Center, speaks of "Maieutic preaching," likening the task of the preacher to that of a midwife: A preacher assists the hearer to bring forth new meaning from the story.

Clearly there is more than rationality involved when a congregation responds to good preaching. The relationship between the preacher and the preached-to is an essential component of what happens. More is involved than meets the eye or strikes the ear.

Where preaching has transforming effect, there is a giving and a taking of power. The one who listens holds power that can be given or withheld. The hearer can give or withhold that power. When it is given, the preacher is freed to go beyond recitation to proclaim truth with authority. In such a case the seed falls on fertile ground. If the hearer chooses to withhold power, holding back from the experience, building walls to close out any communication, the Word will be held back. The seed will fall on barren ground and will fail to bring fruit.

In my experience more hearers are ready to give that power than preachers are to claim it. There is a moment early in the preaching event in which some deep parts of the listener are opened up to the preacher as one is not routinely opened up to a neighbor or a friend or even a spouse. That moment is an invitation to transformation and an opportunity for a dialogue from depth to depth.

If the preacher reaches from authentic depths and touches those open places with real stories of faith, something happens. Transformation can—and does—happen.

All too often we preachers, so insecure in ourselves, are busy explaining why we are there or ingratiating ourselves with a joke or bon mot. Where we succeed, we alleviate our own anxiety; a few people will remember our brilliant repartee, but the moment for transformation may disappear. Preaching is dramatic engagement, not public speaking. The business of preaching is transformation, not transmission of information.

In that dialogue between preacher and listener, the preacher's role as an identified religious leader generally helps the process of transformation, but it is not essential. The fact that the preacher is usually a clergyperson sets this activity apart from ordinary conversation. That religious role sets this piece of communication within a framework of memory, relationship, and expectation that often predisposes the listener to open the inner door, but does not guarantee that the door will stay open for long. Any memory of religious leaders we have known or even heard about affects our openness. Our present and past relationships with pastors, rabbis, and priests perhaps not even of our own faith community will affect our openness. Expectations about what we want and hope for in relationship to God affect how we listen and approach this moment. Our own memory, relationships, and expectations are held there in the preaching moment in the community that surrounds us, where each other listener is bringing those same dimensions of experience to the spoken word.

The result is a moment, perhaps more, of credibility—credibility that has been earned by generations of faithful pastors whose influence continues to lead many listeners to be open to the Word of God, trusting that they will not intentionally be exploited by this particular preacher. That credibility remains, in spite of negative experiences many of us have had with scoundrels masquerading as clergy. That credibility is a precious commodity in every congregation and for every pastor. Where there has been personal exploitation of the congregation or its members by clergy in the past (I am including the sensational material that gets in the papers and also the many less dramatic ways in which clergy may misuse relationships or their position of trust), the new pastor and the people have a major job of rebuilding trust, even for so simple a thing as bringing back power to the preaching ministry. Clergy do more than private damage to themselves and the particular person or people with whom they break this kind of trust; they violate the framework within which gospel can be preached and believed; they fracture the trust that makes it possible for one to speak and another to hear. Where liability can be proved, the worst punishments the courts can mete out are minor compared to the damage to the heart of religious community.

The preaching we know in congregations is ordinarily an activity within the context of worship. But traditionally, preaching has existed as a much larger engagement. Amos preached by using a plumb line to demonstrate God's desire for justice. Jeremiah walked the streets of Jerusalem carrying a yoke on his shoulders to illustrate the fate of the nation if it did not turn from its ways. People of faith have also demonstrated the Word in their actions. The demonstrations organized by Martin Luther King and the SCLC were proclamations of the Word, as are Billy Graham's crusades.

Congregations I know demonstrated the Word by going to South Florida after Hurricane Andrew and repairing houses. My own parish sent a group of young people to Honduras to build screen doors and

install them—this in a place where there were disease-carrying insects and
it was too hot to sleep with a closed door. Many people I know participate in a "grate patrol," handing out sandwiches to homeless people who
sleep on the subway ventilation grates in cold weather.

Although different in many ways from traditional preaching, all
these activities become dialogical. Those who go as the proclaimers of
the Word always are changed by those to whom they "speak." Those
who carry a message discover that they are changed by those who receive it, that power and good news flow both ways.

Yet the ordinary task of preaching belongs in the heart of the congregation. It is one of the givens. It is there, week after week. In the
congregation you must be able to count on this transforming activity
being regularly practiced, regularly available. In God's good time, this
ordinary gift becomes extraordinary.

The effectiveness of the preaching will always have elements of
mystery because of the three parties involved—the listener, the preacher,
and God. Each party has its own personal history and unique relationship to other parties. And of course, the mystery is magnified by the
character of the life of community in the congregation itself.

Mystery is also key to the other primary kerygmatic action of congregations—the act of remembrance, the act of thanksgiving in which
Christians relive the Last Supper. Here also three actors--the participant,
the celebrant, and God—make this a moment of transformation unlike
other transactions. With wide variations in specific theological interpretations of this dramatic action, Christians through the generations have
found that this act places them within the history of salvation in an
unique way, nurturing a life of faith and a commitment to action within
the believer and the believing community. Things happen there that
simply do not happen in other places. Hearts are touched, intentions
formed, commitments made, restorations experienced, foundations re-
discovered, relationships reborn.

In *kerygma* the faith that grounds the church is recounted, spoken,
and re-enacted in such a way that faith comes alive within the congregation.

As *koinonia* is two things at once—a power to support the development of disciples and a sign to society of God's intent that we live in
community—so k*erygma* is both a source of transforming power to those
in the congregation and an impelling force in their encounters with the
outside world.

Didache: The Teaching

Koinonia, kerygma, and now *didache* describe key functions of the congregation as a disciple-making system.[7] None of these functions is fully separable from the others. Teaching occurs in community and its content is the proclamation and stories of the heritage.

In today's churches ministries of teaching inside the congregation stand in urgent need of repair and renovation. Educational ministries may be the most routine deficiency found in congregations. The generations that grew up in the paradigm of Christendom could make assumptions that "everyone" knew what it meant to be a member of the congregation. Today, with even the illusion of Christendom long gone, our educational ministries still assume a population of religious literacy. The level of information about, much less comprehension of, the religious heritage has grown appallingly low. With each generation the level decreases.

The story is told of a relatively recent examination of candidates for ordination. The first candidate was asked, "Who is the patriarch Abraham?" The candidate scratched his head, hesitated, then said, "Wasn't he the first president of the United States who won the Revolution and freed the slaves?" The committee turned warily to the second candidate: "What is the religious meaning of Christmas?" She spoke up quickly, "That's when all the angels make toys for Santa to deliver in the chimneys!" The third candidate was ushered in to a depressed committee. "What happened on Good Friday?" they asked. "Oh yes," the candidate said thoughtfully, "that's when Jesus died on the cross." "Wonderful!" the committee chair said. The candidate warmed to the subject. "And they buried him in a tomb and rolled in a stone for a door." Committee members glowed. "And on the third day they roll away the stone and he comes out. If he sees his shadow, he goes back in and there are six more weeks of winter."

A widespread lack of a grasp of the faith makes it almost impossible for the congregation to establish a set of standards for its teaching ministries or make demands upon its leaders. Without knowledge of the story that sets the religious congregation apart, there is no basis for calling for a different standard by which members are to act. A boundary of knowledge helps members of the community distinguish themselves from the pagan society around them. The establishment of such a boundary is necessary for congregational members to differentiate between the moral and ethical standards of their faith and the customs of the pagan society in which those members live. Equally problematic, this lack of knowledge makes it impossible for parents to nurture their children in their heritage.

We simply must invest major energy across the board to build adult education to bring this generation of adults on board the biblical story and the heritage of faith. We need to expand the network of capable teachers in every congregation. This may be the most important task of the clergy for the next generation.

One area of education is getting some attention—the education for the newcomer or the nonmember. Denominations as well as congregations have recognized that the entry point is a critical opportunity for the new member to be brought into what it really means to belong to this faith-family. The mainline denominations are generally weak in dealing with one particular kind of newcomer—the complete stranger to faith, one not nurtured in a different denominational family. These clergy and congregations tend to have educational systems geared toward nurturing people toward maturity, but they are not very competent at leading people through conversion experiences. This deficit must be filled.

Pastoral care during life-crises has long been a strong suit of congregations and the training of pastoral leaders. Congregations today need to look, however, to the gaps in their sensitivity and caring. Why have people turned outside the church to programs such as AA, Parents without Partners, and the many twelve-step programs? These programs address human needs for care and support that are basically not included in the congregation's menu. In the short run congregations can be grateful for these caring ministries and work to support them and provide them meeting spaces. Doing so will extend the ministries of the congregation, using people who generally know something about the subject. In the long run we need to send our pastoral theologians to school with developmental psychologists, students of social trends, and futurists to analyze the new tensions of modern life and to begin inventing the pastoral care systems that fit the changing needs as congregational members face the crises of new patterns of life.

In all of this, the work of *didache* is to help open up the scriptures, the stories, the lore of the faith so that they are alive and known. When Jesus' life was turned upside down in his encounter with John the

Baptist, his mind held the words of the psalms—memorized from weekly and daily recitation. He had heard stories of the Maccabees from the old people of his village. His mother had taught him strange stories of her own encounters with God. He knew the words of Isaiah and had struggled with their meanings. He had heard other stories from his rabbis. So when his moment of transformation and call occurred, he had at his disposal the words and images to define his vocation and shape his work. He had the raw material ready at hand.

Without such raw material from the rich dialogue of people with the stories of the faith, there really is no community of faith. Without continuous grounding in the story that is the Story, there is no good news for us to pass along. Without continuous grounding in the story, there is no purpose for the congregation, no way to inspire each person to reach out to the bad news that calls each to be a proclaimer of good news. We need congregations in which the words of the psalms and the stories of Jesus are in the ordinary current of life, available as people face daily opportunities, and also when crises occur.

Every congregation must be a center of teaching in an era in which the stories of the faith have slipped away from the consciousness of the wider community. Every adult should be seriously engaged with the scriptures on a week-by-week basis. And each congregation needs to be calling out the teaching skills of more of its leaders so that the story of faith is compellingly presented to the new and the long-term member, the young and the old.

It is the business of the congregation to order its life so that each of us is prepared for our side of the dialogue with the outside world, equipped as Jesus was at the River Jordan—knowing the songs and stories of the faith and ready to respond.

Diakonia: The Serving Role

Few images are more dramatic than that of Jesus washing the feet of his
disciples. Few fit so poorly our image of leadership and authority. Most
of us have real sympathy for Peter's drawing back from a Jesus who
would wash his feet. We are more comfortable with a leader who is
more authoritative and overtly powerful, even though culturally we now
feel more rebellious against such authority than former generations. We
may feel that independent spirit and yet we like to know where we stand,
which means we take some comfort in having an authority who calls the
shots. Peter was right to feel threatened. We, too, are more at ease with
the kind of leader whose feet we must wash than with a leader who
washes ours.

But it is just this image of the servant as leader that we bring as a
gift to our world and as a vocation for ourselves. In Christendom we had
our flirtation with power, sensing that our call was to build empires and
kingdoms shaped by our perception of God's will. We have organized
crusades, waged battles, and built networks of power. We have driven
ourselves and our society to establish the controls of power and law. We
have rarely tried the way of powerlessness, the leadership of servanthood
—in spite of Jesus' clear and often-repeated injunctions. His followers,
he tells us, will become as little children, will serve one another, will
wash one another's feet, will not lord it over one another. Like James
and John, we are more comfortable jostling one another to see who gets
the seats of privilege. Not many of our elections of church leaders fail
for lack of candidates.

How else will they serve? As Jesus demonstrated, by going to the
places of hurt and bringing healing, by going wherever there is bad news
to proclaim good news.

In our time the shape of servant leadership seems to call less for
great crusades of masses of people than the committed actions of disciples, one by one. Crusades were for a time when empires were being
built, when we believed in empires of faith. The message of discipleship
and service today is closer to Jesus' message that the kingdom of God is
within and among you. The task of service is for one transformed heart
to search out the feet that one set of hands is called to wash. One by one.

For congregations this means fewer great campaigns of social
change and more opportunities for each member to discover gifts of

serving and calls for service. My argument is based on the assumption
that each of us is, indeed, gifted for serving and called to specific service.

The task of servant leadership is primarily outside the congregation—in the community that surrounds the congregation. This apostolic
ministry presents special needs for training in the congregation. Within
our congregations, we need more and better understanding of the community. If we intend to serve well, we need the skills of community
analysis and the ability to understand the economic and demographic
trends affecting the world outside the congregation. The servant leader
outside the congregation needs all the skills available to serve in the
ambiguous community world.

In coming years, effective servant leaders will need to draw together
to learn from one another after engagement with the structures of the
society. In time this may become so customary that our ordinary Bible
classes and adult study groups will routinely engage in community
analysis and reflection on work in the community. For now, we probably
need to develop some new educational resources to help servant leaders
find their way in this strange and changing world.

Koinonia, kerygma, didache, and *diakonia*—these, then, are the key
functions that congregations are called to provide for the church of the
future as they have been for congregations of the past.

The Dynamics of Transformation:
From Discipleship to Apostolate and Back

These four functions are needed to bring persons to the fullness of discipleship. We see them as we look inside the church through our imaginary window. If, as I suggested above, we look *out* of our imaginary
window, we see the whole world as quadrants of need, four places in
which people of faith are called to give themselves to the world. The
flow back and forth between discipleship and apostleship continues
throughout one's life, with ever deeper grounding in the life of discipleship.

I diagram the model in this way:

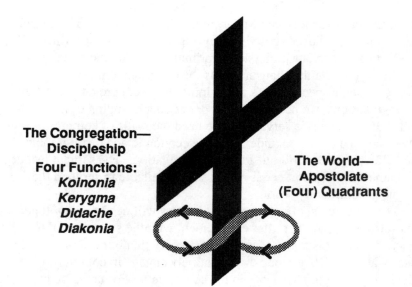

**The Congregation—
Discipleship**

Four Functions:
*Koinonia
Kerygma
Didache
Diakonia*

**The World—
Apostolate
(Four) Quadrants**

All conceptual models violate truth in the attempt to be clear. Certainly this one does, too. But perhaps it can help us see the interrelationship of discipleship and apostleship, the way there is a functional system binding each member to complementary growth as disciple and as apostle.

My assumption here is that every member of the congregation is called to function on both sides of the window, not just one. One "side" is not the prerogative of the clergy or of the laity. Both must interact in such a way that the entire system produces disciples and apostles and continuously reinforces them in faithful serving.

But that is not all. In my diagram, what about the window itself? I want to suggest that for this model the heart of the operation is its dynamic character. It is not enough that the apostolate is built. It is not enough that the discipleship is built. Each depends on interaction with the other; each needs to flow to the other to remain alive. There is a continuous flow from one side of the window to the other. And the heart of the model is the critical transaction as both discipleship and apostleship move through the "window" to enter the other side.

One of the most provocative descriptions of how this congregational dynamic results in transformation comes from Bruce Reed, president of the Grubb Institute of London.[8]

Reed calls his theory the theory of oscillation, building on research and theories in psychodynamics, anthropology, and theology. He describes the process of human living as a continuous cycling back and forth (oscillation) between two poles of dependence. One pole, in which human beings engage the world and its forces, make interventions, and carry out plans, represents life with internalized resources of competence and direction. This is analogous to my category of apostolate, the world outside the window, the world into which the faithful person is sent to respond to pain and need. The other pole represents life when it becomes depleted by the engagement and needs to reestablish its relationship of dependence on its ground of existence. That pole is related to what I have called the inside of the window—the arena of discipleship.

The oscillation between these poles is the story of life, Reed contends. The effectiveness of engaged life grows only out of the ability to depend on strength from beyond oneself. To attempt to live always in the engaged mode is to invite burnout and increasingly ineffective action. To live always in receptivity and dependence leaves one withdrawn from service in the world.

The rhythm of engagement and withdrawal, each leading to the other, is itself the congregation's structure of transformation. The congregation receives its people as they return from a week's engagement with the powers of the world, wherever each has served. Taking those people into the corporate activity of worship gives them back their citizenship in the realm of God and their dependence on God and on each other. The activity of worship once again places them in ordered relationship to the dependability of God and readies them for renewed engagement with the world.

Looking at this model, I see two critical areas for congregational initiative. The congregation needs to see that each member returning from the apostolate is greeted by many opportunities to experience *koinonia, kerygma, didache,* and *diakonia.* The congregation needs to manage the transitions from apostolate to discipleship and from discipleship to the apostolate.

The congregation's responsibility for the apostolate, contrary to modern church discussion, is severely limited. It has a role in helping members analyze the needs of the world and it has a role in helping members reflect on their ministries, but it has little role, corporately, in engaging that world. The temptation to do just that is a major temptation to build religious empires in the model of Christendom. Bruce Reed suggests that such efforts are actually the temptation to secularism— using the tools of the kingdom of this world and rejecting the spiritual tools of the kingdom Jesus proclaimed.[9]

Let me be even more explicit, using an illustration from chapter 2, where I described a map or grid that explores the breadth of ways and styles for being a conveyor of good news. At this point I will illustrate on the grid the "locations" of individual people in a mythical congregation. Each # is the self-selected position chosen by one congregational member. I have used this grid with a number of groups, and although this placement is fictional, it is not unlike the pattern I find typical of many mainline congregations. I discover that congregations with a different orientation often give a quite different profile. Remember, this is attempting to graph one's self-perception of what kind of bad news tends to grab one's attention, and whether one is drawn to act on that bad news through religious or secular structures.[10]

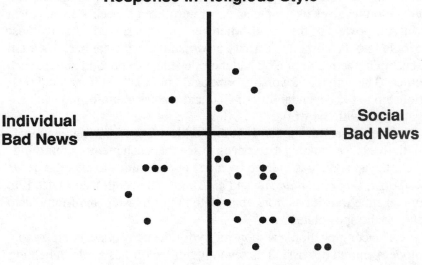

I've found that tracking a congregation on such a grid is valuable for exploring possibilities and relationships, but hardly provides accuracy or predictability. It is a teaching and reflection tool, not a planning tool. Having said that, I find that it helps to discuss how congregations are transformative communities and how that transformation happens. (See the Appendix A for instructions for using this grid to "map" a congregation.)

Where does the mythical congregation I've graphed concentrate? What kinds of bad news would catch attention there and what kinds of programs would such a congregation probably be good at mounting? Conversely, what are the blind spots of that congregation? Where would it be slow to perceive and inadequate in responding to need?

With the majority of people concentrated on the right side of the grid, this congregation will be "at home" in group activities and will understand the need to develop "programs." If this group concentrated heavily on the left side, the question of "programs" would be moot. They would not naturally think about working that way.

This congregation has few members in the upper left-hand quadrant; the largest cluster is in the lower right-hand quadrant, representing those who are grasped by social concerns and tend to seek to deal with them in the secular style.

In such a congregation leaders would probably have natural passion to engage with others to address community concerns—perhaps homelessness or hunger. They would see such engagement as obvious. Necessary. They might have a hard time understanding why everyone did not share the same passion.

In this congregation there is also an obvious low concentration in the upper left-hand quadrant. Those who located themselves there would not be greatly taken with the "majority" passion for programs to alleviate social pain.

Suppose *that* is the quadrant the pastor is attracted to. The pastor's sermons would probably reflect the good news she feels so keenly; the life of prayer and contemplation is the critical good news needed by the community. Many on the board might think of them as "pious" sermons. The pastor might be confused by there being little response to her conviction to feed the life of prayer and contemplation in the midst of the busyness of the community. The board might be more concerned about the need for a solid interchurch council to encourage more low-cost housing and soup kitchens.

The point is that each point on the diagram represents a legitimate but very different understanding of what good news needs to be addressed to what bad news.[11]

The task of the congregation, and consequently the concern of congregational leadership, looks very interesting against this backdrop. Managing the transformation process involves a sensitivity to the diversity of vocations that members feel called to. Unlike models of leadership from an earlier time, the task is not to get all the energy of the congregation focused in one missional thrust but to build as diverse a support system and sending system as possible. In the congregation noted above, leadership should be concerned about what needs to be done to nurture the few in the upper left-hand quadrant. Perhaps leaders should be wondering what such underrepresentation means in the congregation's life. Someone needs to consider how to bring strength to that undeveloped area of congregational life. Does that lack, for example, suggest an area of spiritual blindness?

Managing the moment of transformation from apostleship to discipleship and back again is important if we are to be strengthened to engage the world's bad news. Religious leaders and congregations have no more important task than to help each of us in the movement from discipleship to apostleship and back, continually deepening our awareness of our gifts and of our call. The better that flow, the better each of us will be in proclaiming good news.

All too often we do not have adequate tools to diagnose what we feel called to address or to identify our own personal resources, the gifts and tools available to us through our heritage and faith. Instead of purposeful action, we end up in embarrassed silence or confusion, wishing we could turn the whole thing over to somebody—a pastor—who can deal with it for us.

If our congregations are to help members be transformed from passive onlookers to active participants in communicating God's good tidings, they have large responsibilities in all these areas.

Our congregations have the task of helping members perceive what is going on around them. Being true to the map I have laid out, the need is not only the one liberals have been describing for the past decade—a social analysis of society—but also the one the conservatives have paid lip service to but have not addressed in depth—the spiritual vacuum of humans living in a one-story world. The social analysis of society that our liberals call for sounds like the thinking of sixties radicals dressed up in politically correct language, chasing after the newest trends willy-nilly, paying more attention to *The New Republic* and *Rolling Stone* than to Jeremiah. It has a thin and Godless taste. Similarly, I think the personal analysis of need offered by conservatives is simplistic and narrow, owing more to nineteenth-century morality and piety than to biblical faith.

We need more from each of these families in the churches. Our congregations need to provide much more and deeper engagement in both directions—toward society's transformation and toward personal transformation.

That is their business–helping people find their place in the dynamic of good news, being transformed from passive observers of mission to active participants in it.

This is not a call to activism and it is not a call to contemplation. It is a statement that each of us is called to an engaged ministry in which faithfulness of some will lead to social activity, from do-goodism to advocacy and political action, grounded in our religious heritage. For others it will mean a contemplative or personal involvement with God's purposes for individuals, one at a time. Congregations need to be able to help us find our place in the kind of engagement to which we are called.

Consider again the map of mission above: The point representing each person is best understood as being in orbit around the center, representing the fullness of ministry, with all quadrants active and strong, each part balanced and related to the whole.

There is more. In the map I have shown and the in mythical congregation I used to illustrate my point, each person is symbolized by a particular point on the map. In my experience that is inadequate. That spacial location may hold true at the time, but people change. One's call and response to the call differs from time to time. From our own stories we know that we have grown and changed in how we see and engage in our ministries. So it is for all who seek to proclaim good tidings.

A primary task of the congregation is to be a reliable center around which the variety of its members can orbit, as it were. The stronger the center, the stronger each individual can be in holding true to that moment's sense of call and mission. The stronger and more reliable the center, the more secure the individual can be in exploring new aspects of call and mission. I say even more: The stronger the center, the further out to the extremes in ministry can individual members be encouraged and supported. Perhaps the strongest mission congregations of the future will not be those with the greatest, most visible projects or services, but the ones that can sustain their people in the most diverse and extreme ministries of service and caring one can imagine.

This is a different understanding than most people have of the role of the congregation, but I think it is what is called for in the emerging age. The common understanding, and the source of much congregational strife, is that the task of the congregation is to affirm one place or quadrant on a map as the *right* place, and to program things to encourage everyone to see mission as defined by that position. Clergy tend to think that their conception of the mission is the correct one; they see their job as getting the congregation's program to reflect that sense of mission.

I do not believe the clergy's role has to do with that at all. The clergy have a right to claim a special place within the map of mission, but no right to try to bring the congregation to that place. The clergy's role is to help the congregation establish and hold its center, which is the normative center of the religious tradition in its fullness, not the normative center of that clergyperson's particular vision. The congregation needs so to center its life in its religious grounding that it provides a secure place, able to affirm and strengthen members' various ministries, even those that vary wildly from one another. In this view, a congregation might well be suspicious if it became too uniform in its understanding of mission, if too many began to agree that *real* mission involved perceiving and acting primarily in any one of the quadrants of the map. A pastor's task might well be to try to initiate strength in a quadrant where the congregation is lacking strength, even when it is a quadrant different from where the pastor locates mission.

Holding the center, then, is the task of the congregation. It is a task not of doing but of being. It means exploring and reflecting on the deepest parts of the heritage, experiencing the presence of God, centering in worship, living and breathing the scriptures. It means building an interpersonal community within which each person can be nurtured and strengthened as well as challenged and sent. It means taking very seriously the diversity of God's call to mission, a call that is direct, different, and evolving for each individual. It means taking seriously the complexity and diversity of the good tidings called for by the needs of the world. It means taking seriously the unique set of gifts each person has to mediate between the needs of the world and the good news of God.

I believe that to be a challenging mission for the congregation. Is it, however, a pearl of such great price that we can risk changing the operating structures of our congregations for it? I believe we must.

CHAPTER 4

The Role of the Judicatory

Every congregation is surrounded by denominational structures designed to support and strengthen the total mission of the church.[1] As the storm described in chapter 1 has gathered, and as clarity about what "total mission" actually means, judicatories, like congregations, have found their role confused and uncertain.

In the previous two chapters I have attempted to go to the roots of what congregations need to be about as a first step to our reinventing them for our time. What is true for congregations is also true for the judicatory structures around them. In this chapter I want to begin the conversation about what judicatories need to be for us as we try to weather the storm and reconstruct a church for the next century.[2]

Our Judicatories

Our different denominational groupings and ecclesiological backgrounds give us a hundred ways for congregations to be connected to and communicate with one another. Often we have become so enamored by our own system that we spend our time arguing its superiority or trying to find evidence in scripture that what we inherited through our convoluted history is *really* what God intended in the beginning.[3]

Some of the connectional systems—such as the Catholic and the United Methodist—have clear, sharp delineations of relationship, role, and authority. You can easily find out who makes what decisions and when. When you ask questions, people respond by quoting the book of order. Others—such as the Presbyterian and Episcopal systems—have clear definitions but live with them more casually until there is a fight. Presbyterians will sometimes quote their book of order, but Episcopalians tend to get pretty vague and say, "It must be in the canons somewhere." Still others, such as Baptists and congregationalists, take pride in their independent ways but still find models of community and interrelationship that are mutually supportive. Their habits of relationship and common heritage provide the structure that meets their needs.

Some people are concerned with the collapse of national structures in American mainline denominations. Although I am aware of the difficulties on the national level, I see those problems as being a minor concern when compared to the weakening in the structures of the middle judicatories. Those structures simply are not working well in any of the denominations I'm familiar with. Though less visible than the problem of the national structures, the middle judicatory woes have more pervasive long-term implications. Most of the essential work of the churches —the making and deploying of apostles—goes on without much regard to national policies and directions and could probably survive the demise of those structures without much trouble. That is not so of the regional structures.

Regional middle judicatories are the closest resource to congregations and usually have a responsibility for the care of those congregations. Depending on the denominations, judicatories are given varying amounts of power to intervene in the congregation, but the denominational differences are less than the ecclesiologists claim. Catholic and Methodist systems have clear authority to step into the congregation, where they can do pretty drastic things—remove a pastor or a board or take other disciplinary action. On the other hand, congregationalist denominations give the judicatory very little power for intervention. In fact, for both of these systems, "reality" is somewhere in between the connectional and congregational rhetoric. The quality of the relationship between the judicatory and the congregation speaks volumes about how far the judicatory intervenes. Where little trust exists between judicatory and congregation, Catholic and Methodist bishops know they have been in a fight when they have simply set out to do what they have the legal authority to do. On the other hand, where the trust is high and built on experience, an executive of the United Church of Christ or a Baptist convention can move with more authority than the book allows to help a troubled congregation sort itself out. The in-between denominations, such as the Episcopal and Presbyterian churches, work hard at the trust issue but can get into hot water by making assumptions that the office of the bishop or the authority of the presbytery carries more weight than it does.

The judicatories' accessibility to the congregation is the functional issue I want to focus on. Judicatory offices are relatively close to the congregations. (I see the bishop of Montana and the presbytery executive of Alaska rolling in the aisles at this point. And one judicatory executive in Canada tells me it is nine hours by car from one end of his region to the other!) The judicatory is generally the first office called when there is a crisis of some sort. Judicatories are the first back-up system for congregations.[4]

In choosing to start this discussion by focusing on reconstructing the function of the judicatory, I am obviously excluding two other possible starting points: denominational tradition and organizational precedent. Why do I exclude denominational tradition? Because too often the theological or ecclesiological definition of the judicatory's role has become a religious justification for current organization. If not that, then the language of the heritage has been bent to support structures clearly not envisioned by those who first worked out the meaning of the polity. Why do I exclude organizational precedent? I find that starting there makes it impossible to question the sacred cows of the system. Starting in either of those two places makes it too easy to rationalize what we already do and makes it virtually impossible to initiate change at a base level.

There may be an even more important reason to work at reconstructing our denominational links: This relationship between congregation and judicatory is where the loss of trust most urgently handicaps our religious institutions.

What Congregations Need from Judicatories

Over the past decade I have observed judicatories of many sorts as they tried to provide support to congregations. Each year at the Bishop and Executive Leadership Institute,[5] I have a chance to learn from three or four dozen working executives or bishops. I am deeply indebted to some three hundred of our "alumni" who have shared their wisdom and their

questions. Out of those experiences I have developed a list of what congregations need from judicatories. Rephrased, these functions would
answer this question: What does a judicatory executive need to be good
at? In the spring of 1993 I revised and reworked that list with the help of
a group of Presbyterian executives at a conference at Ghost Ranch. Here
I share this list with you.

Congregations Need Help When They Get in Trouble

Anyone who has worked closely with congregations knows that from
time to time even the best of them get in some kind of trouble.

At The Alban Institute we are particularly conscious of the explosive
fights that break out from time to time in all kinds of congregations for
all kinds of reasons; at this juncture congregations or judicatories often
call on us for help.[7] Church fights break out at unpredictable moments
and can range from minor tiffs to major shoot-outs. We have discovered
that church fights often erupt as a surprise. The people in the congregation may not recognize the conflict for what it is. The pastor may be
away or, worse, may have flipped into panic. Nobody is prepared to deal
with it helpfully. A first symptom of the conflict is often the signing of
a petition about something, followed by a carefully worded ultimatum
from the pastor. Within a brief day or two, the first visible symptom may
have led to all-out war. A judicatory that is alert can often do damage
control and bring the conflict to a constructive outcome.

Church fights are just one of dozens of troubles a congregation
might face. Often enough the denomination's book of order or canon has
procedures for the more common problems, but once again the people of
the congregation often do not know about those procedures. What are
you supposed to do when somebody misappropriates funds? What are
you supposed to do if a major program of the church collapses on you?
What do you do if somebody says you are going to receive a bequest?
What do you do if the highway department wants to build a road through
your church building? What do you do if someone threatens a law suit?
What do you do if the pastor has misbehaved and the board knows it?
What do you do if the pastor has misbehaved and the local paper knows
it? What are you supposed to do if the board cannot get a quorum to do
its work? What are you supposed to do if you suspect the pastor has

become an alcoholic? What are you supposed to do if nobody can find
the official records of the congregation? What are you supposed to do if
a congregation takes a nose-dive in financial receipts?

Others who work with or in congregations will have other items on
their lists. You can be sure of one thing: The list is long. Congregations
can have the same difficulties as any other organization, but the problems
can be exacerbated by two scenarios: (1) a habit of speaking about plain
things in theological double-talk (a screw-up in committee assignments
can become "a violation of my vocational commitments"), and (2) the
likelihood of an appeal to a higher court—God—in a way that escalates a
difficulty into a confrontation of Good and Evil (when you thought you
were just working on the budget!)

Judicatories need to develop a capacity to help congregations clarify
what's at the bottom of the trouble and work out a strategy for dealing
with it. I do not think the judicatory needs to be able to solve the problems. Not at all. But the judicatory needs to have a relationship with the
congregation in which the congregation respects the judicatory and its
advice. In some cases judicatories will have direct answers, but in most
cases they can help most in diagnosing the problem and in advising the
congregation as it deals with the problem or secures other help in doing
so.

Congregations need the judicatory to be clear about what kinds of
situations it can provide help for and what kinds should be referred to
outsiders. Let's be honest. That call is hard for a judicatory to make if it
thinks it must solve everything that comes along or if it has an unrealistic
idea of what its limits of energy and skill are. If a judicatory executive is
insecure or anxious, he may be unable to permit outsiders to help. He is
likely to attempt an in-depth intervention in a two-hour meeting because
that is all the time he can spare. We have found that some kinds of
interventions–a "hot fight," for example—can take six to ten full days of
careful work to move to resolution. In such a case the judicatory executive does not help the congregation by trying to force a quick fix–which
usually exacerbates the problem.

A United Methodist congregation I know asked its district superin-
tendent to help it design a long-range planning process. As he worked
with leaders of the congregation, the DS picked up their anxiety about
mixed signals they were getting from their pastor about his leaving or
staying. The DS was able to help them make a better diagnosis of their

problem so that they could clarify their relationship with the pastor. Then the long-range planning started to get off the ground. That congregation was strengthened by a judicatory executive who dug below the surface issue and helped them deal with a deeper issue.

A Disciples congregation in an urban setting struggled with keeping up a soup kitchen with increasingly burned-out volunteers. When they discussed it with their judicatory executive, she helped them go to other congregations of other denominations and ask for help. The executive also pointed the pastor toward a course in which he could learn more about the care and feeding of volunteers.

These illustrations are deliberately undramatic. But they illustrate the kinds of questions a judicatory has got to recognize as important and be prepared to help a congregation with.

I predict that the stormier the future gets, the more judicatories will have their hands full. Two trouble spots are likely to increase exponentially over the next decade—calls for help in conflict management and with financial short-fall. Judicatories will do well to increase their skills and locate trustworthy allies in these two areas--people who can be called in to add to the available resources. They need to have a large "adjunct staff—people whose salaries they do not pay, but whom they can call in for "piece work." That is one of the most productive roles The Alban Institute plays, backing up the energies and skills of judicatory leaders.

From time to time, congregations need help. Judicatories need to be ready to provide counsel and/or resources.

Congregations Need to Be Left Alone

For the most part, when congregations are not actively asking for help, judicatories need to leave them alone. Most congregations have programs in place and energy harnessed to their tasks. Most congregations have a pretty good working relationship with their pastors.

If such is the case, congregations ought to be left alone most of the time to get on with their work. I state this inelegantly as my *bias toward neglect*. Perhaps I would not have such a bias in other generations, but now is the time....

Judicatories often operate as if they were being remiss if they are not calling a lot of meetings, working with a lot of task forces, and sponsoring many judicatory activities for laity and clergy to be engaged in. Most congregations do not need it.

I get nervous around judicatories that are tooling up to develop mission statements and long-range strategic plans. Maybe it is a good idea sometimes, but maybe it is organizing to do something nobody needs to have done. The person being served in much judicatory activity is the judicatory itself or its staff members who need to exercise their creativity.

My point here is to encourage a judicatory to operate strategically in terms of its primary task—strengthening the congregations within its bounds. That means not treating all congregations alike, but differentiating among them—being prepared to make strong interventions where needed, and to leave others alone.

Congregations Need to Be Jacked Up When They Are Off Base

Congregations need somebody who cares enough about them to tell them when they are genuinely off base. When poverty abounds in their neighborhoods, somebody needs to raise questions if they plan opulent new buildings. When children and families are at risk, congregations need to be brought up short if they drop day-care centers on which their communities have come to rely or pull out of coalitions for family aid or support for the public school systems. Congregations need to be called to account if they neglect opportunities to support mission efforts outside their own local programs. Congregations need to be jacked up when they are irresponsible in their rebellion against their own denominational structures. Congregations need to be called to account when they misuse their staffs or pay subminimum wages. Congregations with significant financial resources need help learning to be good stewards. Warning: They probably will not accept help from the judicatory itself. (They probably do not trust the judicatory, often for good reason.) This means the judicatory needs to be sure they have access to resources the congregations will trust.

When I say congregations need somebody to hold them accountable, I do not mean that the judicatory should see itself as calling the shots in all the areas described here. The point is that somebody needs to get involved, ask questions, if necessary put congregations on the defensive, and make them think through what they are doing. If they take time to reflect, check their status and direction of their mission, and then go ahead, I think the judicatory has done the job called for. I do not believe the judicatory has the responsibility of always being right or even obeyed.

Congregations Need Pastoral Care

I speak here about the corporate pastoral care that congregations need in their life together. Of course the pastor has a task here, but some things need another dimension of care.

Congregations need grief-care when facing the loss of a pastor or a key lay leader. Congregations need care when the building burns down or is flooded. Congregations need care when a big local business goes belly-up or a local catastrophe strikes--a hotel burns down or a plane crashes. The congregation needs pastoral care after a fierce congregational battle. Congregations need lots of care when they have been betrayed by the misbehavior of a clergyperson. They may even need care when there is prominent misbehavior by a clergyperson of another congregation, even in another denomination.

Good pastoral caregivers often see needs those needing care do not see. Pastors recognize grief and need to be aggressive in "moving in," even though the grieving person may not "want" attention. Pastors know that sometimes withdrawal is a sign of depression. Similarly, judicatory executives need to be willing to be a bit pushy when they know help is needed—such as when a pastor leaves and grief hits the congregation. This is one place (there are others) where congregations cover over their feelings with all sorts of self-important verbiage—like the child who tells the parent, "I can do it myself." Parents need to be on the lookout for the child who is involved in something he really cannot handle by himself and be willing to step in. So, too, with judicatory executives and bishops and their staffs.

My focus on the negative experiences that trigger a need for care should not negate the need for the judicatory to be there for the moments of celebration and the marking of milestones. There are times and communities that need a message of congratulations when the high-school team wins—or comes in second–in the state basketball tournament. Or even when a fund drive goes over the top.

Congregations Need Pastoral Care for Their Pastors

No one needs to underline the pressure pastors are under today. As paradigms of ministry change, clergy are also buffeted by financial pressures, insecurity regarding their professional futures, and a diminished public image of their role in society.

The multiplicity of changes that have simultaneously hit clergy leave them stressed and feeling burned out as they try harder to accomplish their work with reduced resources. All too often I find clergy almost immobilized–they are so aware of their pain and need. When in that state, they forget what they have learned in pastoral care—that pastoral care does not equal pats on the back and hand-holding.

The pastoral care clergy need from their judicatories is the kind that gets them to be the first-class professional leaders they intend to be. I have worked with clergy for decades, and I find them happiest tackling their work, solving problems, making their bricks whether or not anybody gets them the straw. Judicatories need to avoid infantilizing their clergy, thinking of them as "poor sweet babies" needing constant care. Clergy, like everyone else, can become bottomless pits of needs if their leaders pander to those needs.[8]

Judicatories do need to be aware of the heavy stresses and try to see that resources are available for the clergyperson temporarily overwhelmed, seriously depressed, or ill. But I would urge a *bias toward health*, giving clergy additional challenges and resources, not sympathy. Even where there are difficulties, clergy need to be encouraged to take action for their own health. Having a good list of opportunities for professional education and a solid scholarship fund is more important than planning a clergy development program that is fully funded by the judicatory.[9]

We do need to recognize the extraordinary pressures on clergy. The older they are, the more revolutions they have lived through. What is expected of them has changed 180 degrees. Once the front-line troops of a crusade, they have become the mess sergeants in an army they do not control. Their role as community leader often has been eroded. The clarity about their work has disappeared. They catch more criticism than previous generations of clergy. Most of them were trained for another role, another institution, another history, another world.

Judicatories exercise pastoral care by helping these dedicated people pull up their socks and stockings and pitch in as the competent learners they can be.

Congregations Need Help with Leadership Development

Many congregations do not adequately train new leaders and see to effective leadership transitions—for laity or clergy. The most serious gap is in the inadequate training support judicatories give when clergy and lay leaders are starting up a new leadership team. Every judicatory needs to give priority to ensuring that every pastor moving into a new position has training or consultative assistance to put together a new working team of clergy and laity. I see this as the most strategic opportunity to raise the level of effective leadership in a congregation. Every judicatory needs to have such a program in place every year. It should be a built-in expectation. At The Alban Institute we have helped Episcopalians and Lutherans begin such programs.

A lesser opportunity is available every year when new board members are selected for the congregation; every such change is an opportunity for new team building for the congregation leadership.[10] Most congregations are left to fend for themselves at these transitional times, with the result that few congregational boards operate very effectively. Large congregations need team building and training for their staffs. Even though they have resources at hand, they often forget to do it. Judicatory executives need to push them to act on this need. If there are several such congregations in the judicatory, annual or biannual staff-building conferences can be very helpful.

Small congregations may have limited ability to train leaders. Some fail to see the community benefits of such training. In many smaller communities, the church-based leadership training is virtually the only leadership development available in the whole community. The Alban Institute has found that when we work with a small-town church to resolve conflict, the whole community gains resources for dealing with other conflicts. Leadership training in communication skills, in how to manage small groups, in how to design effective meetings, in how to put together an educational design—all are needed in every congregation. Yet only the largest megachurches have the resources to do it for themselves.

Some judicatories have been able to broker the training resources available in larger congregations for use in smaller ones. Large congregations often have more staff resources than does the judicatory.

Congregations Need Technical Assistance

Many congregations have limited resources of technical know-how in managing their own lives or interacting with the outside community.

Basic planning skills and knowledge about how institutions work are important for congregations in changing times. For instance, techniques for fund raising and fund management can help congregations order their lives, but someone has to see that those resources are available. Some of the issues addressed earlier in this chapter have to do with technical assistance—knowledge about conflict management, for example, or understanding the impact of grief on corporate groups.

Congregations often also need help from outside to understand what is going on in the world in which they minister. Few of them have skills in reading demographic or economic trends in their town or county. Information and interpretation is often available, but they do not know how to access it. Someone "outside" may have to help congregations connect with this knowledge if it is to help them with their ministries. A judicatory office that has a list of phone numbers of county planning agencies in each county can really help its congregations that want to plan for the future.

Most congregations also need a great deal of help in professional techniques for fund raising. Few congregations are able to give members adequate help in planned giving, but judicatories can locate such resources and make them available.

Congregations Need a Sense of Their Place in a Larger Mission

Too many congregations get locked into the local sense of mission
with such enthusiasm that they turn their backs on needs beyond their
boundaries. This is both good and bad: good in that it often is a new and
important commitment of direct, hands-on, grass-roots action that pro-
ceeds from their faith; bad in that it disengages them from mission concerns that genuinely belong to them and have a claim on them.

The judicatory has a special responsibility to help the congregation
widen the horizon of its concern for mission. The judicatory has a difficult, slippery path to follow—pushing congregations to respond to more
distant mission responsibilities, while not using that simply to justify the
judicatory budget. Much of the suspicion of congregations toward their
denominational structures comes from a discomfort that all the talk about
"mission" is just a ploy to garner money to pay bureaucrats. Or, what
may be more destructive of trust, that the judicatory is just interested in
its own pet projects, most of which do not look like mission to the people
in the pew. This has dug us into a hole in which even the most high-
minded pleas of church leaders are likely to find considerable suspicion
among many generous contributors who care for mission and care for the
church. In such a climate, judicatories dig even deeper holes when they
hold ever bigger and more frequent "extra mission giving" campaigns in
which they disguise the fact that they are raising money to continue
doing what people have decided they are not enthusiastic about doing.

Even though past practices have damaged trust and credibility, judicatories have a responsibility to work at widening the vision of the local
church. So they have to rebuild trust. That's not a bad thing to be working on. If the judicatory does not help the congregation look beyond its
bounds, it will be damaging the congregation. Yes, the task is difficult
and there are patterns from the past that will haunt us. No matter. I do
not suggest a bias toward inaction.

Congregations Need Someone Who Listens and Listens and Listens

The most important thing a congregation needs may be somebody outside who just listens and pays attention. Someone who reads its weekly
bulletin and picks up signals. Someone who knows the group well

enough to recognize when it needs some kind of intervention. Someone
who is not afraid to follow up on hunches that things are not going well
or—perhaps—when things need celebrating.

I have, then, good news and bad news for those who work in judicatory offices, whether they be bishops, executives, regional/area ministers,
superintendents, moderators, or... some name I haven't yet heard.

The bad news is what most of you already know in your bones. The
old system is not working. It is based on organizational assumptions and
functions designed for another age and another way of thinking. It is
based on sets of loyalties and understandings of authority that do not
hold today. What may be worse, the financial underpinnings of the judicatory are threatened almost everywhere, and that threat will not be dealt
with adequately by working harder at the no-longer-working system.

I hope I am being very clear that the bad news is very bad and very
urgent. The effectiveness of every regional judicatory I know is in serious trouble and it is not getting better. I dramatize my point by asking
judicatory executives how they will do their jobs in five years when they
have half the staff they have now. I ask them where their successors will
get salaries from.

The good news is good news indeed. The need for what a judicatory
can provide is sharp and real, even if it may be different from the functions called for in past generations. It is also true that the functions are
needed by the part of the system that has the resources to pay the costs–if
convinced that the functions are focused on helping mission happen. The
connection between congregations and judicatories is of enormous self-
interest to each–not simple selfish self-interest, but a self-interest in
seeking to carry out their call of faith, to make a difference in the world
and for the kingdom of God.

William McKinney, widely known teacher, leader, researcher,
and consultant who works at Hartford Seminary, was recently asked to
analyze the role played by people who worked regionally in a project
(run by the Center for Congregations in Community Ministry at
McCormick Seminary in Chicago) to support local congregations as they
got involved in social ministry projects in the Midwest. These support
people were not acting as judicatory executives, but I see McKinney's
findings as being useful to our judicatory discussion: McKinney described their role as that of "persistent friends." These people worked for
the project but were external to the congregations, bringing skills and

challenges to them. They prodded the congregations, advised the congregations, "held hands" with the congregations, helped the congregations find resources, found ways for them to overcome divisions and conflicts, showed them how to plan, and also stood by and watched. They did not give up on the congregations when they got in self-defeating patterns. They kept coming back and coming back, calling the congregations to higher expectations.

Yesterday's models, in which executives acted as if lording it over congregations was the best way to help them, work in fewer and fewer places. They no longer generate loyalty or produce results as they did in a different world. Similarly, the models in which the executives stood back only to come in—with apology—when blood was on the walls do not do justice to the critical developmental needs congregations have today.

We can clarify the executive role only as we understand the life of congregations and the functions needed if congregations are to be engaged in their work of reaching out into human lives and communities. This chapter has been an attempt to begin looking at those functions "from the ground up."

McKinney's phrase "persistent friend" is a good place to start. The model of those Chicago project leaders is instructive. As long as there are congregations that seek to make disciples and send them into the community as bearers of good news, those congregations will need persistent friends who challenge and support them in their task.

CHAPTER 5

Roadblocks and Directions for the Journey

Those of us who seek to reinvent our religious structures for the next generation are aware of the complex and resistant forces we face.[1] It often seems that when we take one step ahead, we slip back two. Our "new project" ends up putting us in more trouble than we were in before. How many important attempts have been made in how many creative ways? And yet the winds of the storm are unabated. We sometimes wonder if our sheer stubbornness keeps our hopes alive.

I cannot number the wise and committed colleagues I have seen charge up the hill, year after year, all with conviction, most with great plans, all absolutely certain that this time, this time, they would succeed. I hear that conviction in the voices of those who phone me to tell of the great plan they have developed—and I remember how excited someone was thirty years ago who tried that very plan in Chicago or in the Bay Area. I have a memory bank full of failed efforts. None failed because of stupidity. None failed because of lack of faith.

Perhaps we underestimated the problems that stood in the way. Perhaps we underestimated the power of the Opposition. Perhaps we were naive. I have a feeling that one of our most powerful idols is "My New Idea," "The New Program," or even "The New System." Martin Marty once told me that my work with congregations had reminded him "that there are no big deals any more."

Some of us have no choice but to charge up that hill again. As Luther put it in a more overtly theological sense, we "can do no other." And what can we begin to do that is different? We can more consistently try to learn from our experience and map out those forces that consistently get in our way. In this chapter I want to name some of the major impediments ahead of us and the clues I have for moving ahead. I am aware that many of the obstacles are connected to the others. We are unlikely to be able to solve them one by one; we will have to deal with the whole system at once.[2]

We Have Dug Ourselves into a Financial Hole

One of the major prophets of the twentieth century is a shadowy figure described by Woodward and Bernstein in their story of Watergate. Deep Throat, as they named the man who spoke from the shadows of the parking garage, said, "Follow the money!" They did, and they brought down a president.

Deep Throat's advice to the reporters is a guideline for looking at problems and directions in any institution; it has great relevance for the difficulty we have in dealing with congregations and in trying to change them. Let's discuss several areas in which our relationship to money is crippling our ability to do what we say we want to do to renew our institutional life. Leaders of churches, especially clergy, use language all the time, often to obscure rather than clarify. But here I will use unvarnished language, saying things more directly than in our churchy style. Forgive me if I offend.

We Have Consistently Misappropriated Funds

I probably have your attention. The point is that churches consistently use large amounts of money in ways the donors do not understand or approve of.

There is no criminal intent. This is what happens: Those who give to their congregations do so for a variety of motives and in a variety of styles—from those who "pay their dues" to those who want to "make an impression" to those who give in simple gratitude to God. But there is an implicit contract in all cases that the resources will be used to support the purposes and concerns of the religious community. People who give to churches expect that the money will be used for the purposes—the mission—of that church. Not many people who give do so stating narrow restrictions, although some do. Most people are prepared to trust their leaders and give some latitude in how the funds are spent. They know that it may be important to support some things they are not enthusiastic about. They expect that their money will be used to make a difference in something important.

But in the past few generations a gap has grown between what "mission" means to the spenders of the money and the givers of the money.[3]

I first saw this misappropriation in action some years ago as a parish pastor in North Carolina in a judicatory that prided itself on the forward-looking and extensive ministry it supported in the regional universities and colleges. We had clear plans to place a full-time college chaplain in as many key places as possible. The area had many fine institutions of higher learning, parents of college students were in all the congregations, and few parishes had any questions about support for this vital work. What happened? Over a relatively short period of time, the function of the college chaplains changed. At first college chaplaincy was basically a one-on-one pastoral ministry not unlike youth ministry in a congregation. Then, responding to pressures and needs they discovered on campus, chaplains began to work at ministry to educational, institutional structures and then at ministry to structures of society. In many ways this was a requirement of the time—the sixties—when to be in touch with student life one had to be concerned for the issues that engaged students. College chaplains, if they were to be in touch with their students, felt they had to be counseling groups that were planning demonstrations and getting out "where the action was," not planning church suppers and liturgies and visiting dorm rooms.

The hindsight of a few decades makes it easy to argue for or against that change of "job description." Some things were gained, others lost. That is not the point. This is: The supporters of college ministries thought that they were supporting the older model of ministry. At annual convention after annual convention, support for college ministry was called for by denominational leaders *who themselves knew that the work had changed, but those leaders did not mention the changes to the laity.* Many of the donors did not know the change had occurred.

Often the donors discovered the change by reading a newspaper account of a college chaplain making a speech in the middle of a controversial meeting or demonstration. More than one chaplain got fired. Many donors felt betrayed. Other donors—probably the majority—recognized the change and came to accept it but lost a little trust in the system. The people who had the power to set the policy did not work at helping the donor understand how the mission had changed.

What I have described here in one small story about college ministry has been happening for a generation in many other areas of mission work. Denominational and regional leaders have genuinely struggled to find more effective ways to do the work of ministry, developing imaginative and important new directions of mission. But they have allowed terrible gaps to develop between what they are doing and what the donors think they are doing. To the donor, such a gap can feel like betrayal of a trust.

The point is not whether their programs were right. (My bias is that most of the efforts have been well motivated and on target.) The point is that we have allowed gaps to develop that have eroded trust.

The public media occasionally step into this gap to the dismay of religious leaders. Every decade or so *Reader's Digest* publishes an article about what the World Council of Churches or the National Council of Churches or one or another of the denominations is *really* doing with the donations it receives. "The people in the pew" give a loud cry because they have not known that their church leaders have changed programs. The church leaders get equally upset, thinking that important mission concerns are being undercut. Both have a point. But again, my point lies in the fact that our religious leaders have not felt accountable for their choices. In their enthusiasm for important mission initiatives, they have acted like intellectual elites. At their worst, some of them have actually felt contempt for the narrow vision of some of the donors, and they have felt justified in using the funds in ways those donors would never support.

The prophetic task of the church often requires some to step out beyond the common denominator of understanding. But prophets understand that there is cost to that stepping out, and they have to expect to pay it. Many people expect denominational leaders to exert prophetic leadership, but no one seems to understand that prophets rarely have been known to lead institutions. Samson is rightly honored as a prophetic judge, but look what happened to him when the walls fell down on him. I sometimes call this pattern of denominational use of funds the Samson syndrome of leadership. It may do some damage to the Philistines, but it's hard on the prophet, too.

Our problem? Our way of operating has led to significant loss of trust in our systems.

We Refuse to Pay Attention to the Disaster That Is Approaching

Congregations and their religious systems have their heads in the sand in terms of their future support. I see a brick wall thirty years down the pike. I don't hear anybody else talking about it.

All of the evidence we have points in one direction: Younger generations do not contribute to religious institutions as generously as did their elders. Published studies of the philanthropic giving of baby boomers are not encouraging, although a few optimists hope that their behavior will change when the mortgage is paid up and tuition payments have come to an end.

I see little evidence that the denominations are exercised about this problem or being aggressive in trying to overcome it. With all the professed desire for expanding the diversity of the churches, denominations are avoiding the problem of research and development of ways to increase giving among a more diverse range of groups and givers.

More than that, the donor base of the mainline denominations continues its dependence upon a monochrome constituency—white, middle-aged or older church members. The donor base is aging and is not expanding in numbers, diversity, or age. This alone shakes my confidence in our denominational leadership. It is one thing to try to change things and fail; it is another not to try.

In the foreseeable future, demand for financial resources is likely to continue to outstrip "supply." Indeed, I believe financial resources will continue to diminish. In times of diminishing resources, any project, program, or ministry that is not self-supporting will be in trouble. Subsidies of any kind will be hard to come by. Church leadership will increasingly be concerned with staff and program cuts. Inevitable cutbacks will always engender conflict between those whose priorities differ. We already see this being worked out in hundreds of judicatory budget debates and in all the national denominational debates.

There is some good news and some bad news in the reliance of our institutions on their proven donor base.

The good news is the growth of strong pledged annual giving over the past generation. Mainline church members now talk about proportional giving and even tithing. An increasing number practice one or the other. Some mainline denominations, like mine, the Episcopal Church, have experienced remarkable growth of pledged giving with strong leadership from the top down and from the bottom up.

Some of the bad news is related to that. Most of our denominations are so dependent on this single source of funding that they put all their fund-raising energy into it. They seem to pay little attention to the fact that the pool of givers is declining, making this a short-term strategy. Their success keeps them from developing other approaches. The denominations seem to have forgotten that pledging itself is a relatively recent practice. All the eggs seem to be in that one basket. Other baskets are needed.

The most perplexing neglect is of planned giving.[4] Denominations and congregations that are strong in support of tithing blanch when the word *endowment* comes up. I wonder why it is so salutary to give 10 percent of one's salary to one's congregation and at the same time so dangerous to give 10 percent of one's estate to the congregation. There seems to be a theological position of some sort staked out on the old saw, "The only way to kill a church is to give it an endowment." Clergy, almost to a person, are energetically suspicious of endowments. Few clergy are open to their parishioners who want to leave substantial sums to their congregations. Few of us seem to realize that for most of its history most of the church was financed primarily through resources gained by bequest. A few judicatories and congregations have appointed planned-giving officers, but lack of interest in their work tends to marginalize them and decrease their effectiveness.

While I have never heard of a seminary, a college, a hospital, or even a symphony orchestra saying, "We would be unfaithful to our traditions if we accepted resources for the future! (the only healthy hospital is one whose patients bear the full load of the costs)," I hear that regularly from congregations and from clergy. The situation may be worse. I know of seminaries (with aggressive development programs) that teach students that endowments are bad for congregations. The same seminaries have aggressive planned giving programs for their own support.

Congregations (or judicatories) with significant endowments do have some special challenges.[5] Managing the endowment itself takes energy. There are big—and different—problems of priorities. Stewardship education is difficult in such congregations. More than a decade of working with endowed congregations has helped me see that the problems they face are formidable. I cannot understand why this so frightens most church leaders. It is as if church leaders, particularly clergy, assume that money itself is evil—a strange theological position for those whose scriptures include the story Jesus told about the talents. I can understand anxiety about a difficult task; I cannot excuse the cop outs I see in this area.

The fact is that *all* congregations are endowed already. Some of them are heavily endowed even though they do not admit it. They have buildings given them by past generations. (Often the current users of the building are noted only for the fact that they are inadequately maintaining that endowment.) They have forms of organization and a heritage of faith that is an endowment from past generations. They have a story of ministry that they did not invent. Even most with treasurers and boards who plead "poor mouth" have a certificate of deposit or two stored away somewhere or a sizable "reserve fund."

Their fear of "admitting" their endowment is instructive. It suggests how threatening it is to admit one's gifts. It also suggests that one can avoid responsibility and accountability if one denies the giftedness.

Neglecting planned giving is bad enough, but we have more on our heads.

This generation of church members has spent up the endowments of previous generations. Former generations, loving their churches and acting in good faith out of the best insight they had, built an infrastructure for that church's mission.[6] The infrastructure includes great buildings for worship. Former generations recognized the need for church-affiliated seminaries, colleges, and schools. They built great national commissions and boards to shape mission effort. None of it was easy. And they built them for us.

Our generation is using up those gifts, spending them prodigally. Of course those who went before made mistakes in what they thought we might need. They did not know that we would have a hard time paying the heat bills for some of the stone monsters they built. But what gifts they tried to set aside for us! They built for the future they thought we had in store. Our generation seems intent upon complaining about their mistakes and dismantling the infrastructure they built. We have built very few institutions for the next generation. In former generations, some would have torn down the inappropriate buildings and built better ones. We sit around and complain.

Instead of making provision for the church for future generations, this generation of church leaders is being prodigal with the gifts of the past. It is only in the church's institutions of education that I see signs of awareness that funds for the future must be generated. (In those institutions I suspect that the energy for seeking endowments comes from their roots in the financial quagmires of higher education rather than their heritage in the churches.)

We do not have much time to do a turnabout. In 1993 Larry Carr, president of the Presbyterian Foundation, said that within the next seventeen years $6 *trillion* will change hands, as one generation's resources are passed along to the next. This will be the largest transfer of resources in history. That means that in those seventeen years the most generous supporters the church has ever had will be among those whose resources will pass to other hands. Within the next two decades, the current generation of tithers will be replaced by a generation that has not yet been convinced that tithing is a good idea.

Unless we change our behavior radically, our current generation of generous supporters of the church will be told to take their gifts elsewhere. If the churches ever had an opportunity to develop resources for the future, the time is now. The time is not likely to return. The clock is ticking.

I see almost no one in the churches paying any attention. We are not suffering from some inevitable decline of resources; we are committing institutional suicide. It is what Elisabeth Kubler-Ross called denial.

Continuing this head-in-the-sand approach will be disastrous financially. It is even worse when we realize that our avoidance of this issue also represents our avoidance of every American Christian's primary spiritual problem—being wealthy. Here I am making the case for the institutional problem we have. There is a deeper problem more directly related to our mission. Our avoidance of this issue is part of a larger avoidance at the heart of our spiritual task as churches. Almost all Americans are rich. Even our poorest are infinitely better off than the poor elsewhere in the world. A primary spiritual task of churches is to help Americans deal with the dilemmas of wealth. Our avoidance of the issue of endowments is a symptom of our avoidance of that larger spiritual task. A church that cannot face the sin and grace involved in endowments is crippled in dealing with the sin and grace with which every one of its members has to live daily. Here I am not arguing that great issue. I am speaking to the narrow institutional concern: We are committing institutional suicide.

We Have Failed to Enfranchise the Laity

The laity has never had institutional power in the churches.[7]

Let me defend that overstatement. Most people in Protestant denominations point to significant areas in which the laity does, indeed, have great power within the institution. Some of those denominations can point to historical moments or even legal entitlement today that support assertion of power by the laity, sometimes at the most critical points of the institution's life. I do not deny those arguments. I do not deny that laypeople do frequently shift the balance and affect the outcome around issues under debate. But churches are institutions the ordinary operations and decisions of which are guided by clergy. Churches are clergy-run organizations.

It is a situation comparable to this: The justice system in this country is a lawyer-run operation. Or this: The medical system is run by doctors. In neither case am I saying that the system is necessarily bad— just that each is run by the professional group that has the most at stake in the arrangements of the system.

Most of us know extraordinary lawyers who live sacrificial lives to build a just society in which everyone is treated well under the law. Most of us know doctors who have given their lives and health to bring healing to others. That's not the point. The legal system, the justice system, is run by lawyers who make a living from the law. Over time the rest of us have begun to wonder if that system, as it is played out in American life, really is a system that we can trust to operate for the benefit of those who are not lawyers. Similarly more and more people are wondering if our medical system is working to the benefit of the public and if the decision making should continue to be ruled by those who stand most to benefit from it.

Large questions are being raised across our society about both of these areas. The laity has never had power in the legal system. Perhaps the legal system is too important to too many people to be left in the hands of lawyers. The laity has never had power in the health system. Perhaps the health system is too important to too many people to be left in the hands of doctors.

Our society has not yet come clear about either of these questions, but there is a growing awareness that the decisions made in the past in both those systems have not turned out to be as good for society as they have been for lawyers and for doctors.

I could point to an even more dramatic illustration. As a nation we have begun to wonder if it is wise to let those who are organized to promote the use of guns make national policy about guns in the hands of the public. Years ago when our government was being formed, we became clear that war and defense was too important to allow policy to be made by the generals; we mandated political leadership for our war efforts.

The churches' power system has grown into what we now call clericalism. It is a power system that has grown up because it made religious institutions strong and effective over the centuries. But it has become a system that is so busy protecting the past that it no longer serves the future. It is a power system in which the primary decisions about the churches' futures are made by the professional class that has the most at stake in those decisions professionally, personally, and financially. In other situations we call this conflict of interest. The self-interest skews the institution toward the concerns of the clergy. We need to know that some people look suspiciously at our rules about minimum salaries for clergy, our subsidy of clergy training, and our definition that the minimal congregational framework include one paid clergyperson. I have heard it said that the church sometimes operates primarily as an employment system for clergy.

I am saying this as bluntly as I can. I do not for a moment deny the quality of the clergy I know. Of course there are bums and charlatans in the crowd, but I know more, thousands more (I mean that literally!) who are self-giving and live out a dedication that inspires me. I admire no professional class more for its contributions to building community and touching human lives. I claim that professional class as my own, and I am proud of it.

But some part of me knows a more complex reality. The decision-making processes of religious institutions are mostly controlled by clergy. I am not talking about the specific voting processes or the genuinely democratic intent of church leaders and clergy. I am talking about the arrangements around the voting—the way clergy are paid to go to denominational meetings year after year, gaining expertise and power in the system. I am talking about the way clergy are leaned on and trusted for advice by lay delegates. I am talking about the systems of rotating membership on congregational boards, a system that effectively destroys lay power in favor of the clergy. I am talking about the "old boy" systems from seminary into which women clergy are only beginning to find their way and which shape so many appointments to decision-making roles. I am talking about the way the professional class systematically draws key lay leaders into itself, sending them off to seminary to be co-opted into the power class. I am talking about the way clergy can afford to be there at the midweek meetings when the decisions are made. The arrangements multiply their power.

Few of the clergy I know, and probably none of the extraordinary clergy I know, believe in or want the kind of power I have described in the last paragraph. Most of them abhor such self-serving interpretations of what the system does.

Which is my point. This is a power system that is larger and more powerful than the people in it. It is a set of customs and arrangements grown up through the years that one person has little power to change. It is the kind of demonic power that Saint Paul warns against when he talks about "principalities and powers" (Eph. 6:12 KJV). There is a key truth about such powers when they are uncontrolled. All of them draw their power from the good in them, but good becomes demonic. Lucifer, we must remember from our mythology, was the most beautiful of the angels, which made him the most powerful when he fell to become the Adversary.

The development of clergy over the centuries has been one of the greatest achievements of the churches. Clergy have been at the heart of the growth of theologies and schools and sacrificial living of all kinds. Each of us has been nurtured by our relationship with great clergy.

That is precisely why clericalism is so powerful. When clergy become a power system, the system is clericalism. It takes power and authority unto itself, away from the church it is intended to serve. That makes it demonic.

The same can be said of any *ism*. Our usual problem with understanding this simple spiritual truth is that we generally *like* some of these demons. In our common parlance, we disapprove of bad demons such as racism, sexism, ageism, and we excoriate those who act in their power. But not the demons we like! All the "political correctness" talk is about how we choose certain demons to attack, while harboring our own demons as personal pets.

The church of the future must break the power of clericalism. The continuation of decision making based on the welfare of one professional group will be financially and organizationally disastrous. More than that, it will increasingly focus clergy as functionaries in a dysfunctional institution, when we need clergy who can lead us with religious authority.

The church of the future needs clergy who can lead us into deep places, who can teach us the enduring story of the people of God. We do not need them to be managers of an institution.

Clergy by themselves cannot and will not relinquish their power. There will be no change until the laity takes the lead. The church is too important to be left in the hands of the clergy.

We Have Built Unhealthy Dependency Systems

Over the generations institutions and groups within the churches have become stratified into levels of power. As in most historic institutions, those stratifications became hierarchical, with those considered most important at the top and those less important at the bottom. Who knows how it got started? Some read the development as part of a conspiracy of males to dominate females. They may be right. Some read it as a dialectic of history. They may be right. Some read it as a simple functional development of society. They may be right.

Wherever it came from, it leaves some obvious problems for those who want religious institutions to weather the storms of change we have described. There are emotional overtones to the hierarchical structures that developed in the churches, overtones that complicate our concern to make the structures more responsive to today's needs.

One of the simplest and most helpful insights into this structural problem was given by Thomas Harris, in his book *I'm O.K.–You're O.K.*, a popular self-help book of several years back.[8] In that book, Harris used our familial experiences as children and parents to describe patterns of reaction in dependency systems. I want to use his model to point to similar patterns in the hierarchical structures of churches.

Harris reminds us of the characteristic messages we received from parents—commands or exhortations to do something we usually did not want to do. He describes those messages, collectively, as a set of tapes we record in memory. The tapes say things such as: "Clean your plate. Put on your galoshes. Don't ever do that again! Stop that! Behave yourself. Sit still and listen. Do what you are told." Most of us can add to the list from our experience.

Those collective experiences are recorded in our memory, Harris suggests, as our own memory-cassette of "parent tapes." He suggests that they become the emotional framework we use in dealing with our own children. When push comes to shove in our relationship with those dependent upon us, we usually flip back to use those remembered tapes.

Hold on. There's more. In response to the parent tape, the child develops a set of emotional—and verbal—answers: "I don't want to. I won't. Make me. It's not fair. Jimmy doesn't have to, why should I? You can't make me."

Those become our "child tapes." Harris says these tapes go underground in our consciousness but pop out at unexpected places. We may be secure professional adults but when a fellow worker says, "You better get that report in on time," a dormant child tape is triggered to feel *says who?* We actually respond with something like "You don't have authority to give me that assignment!" Acting out of remembered emotions, we give a rational version of a childish response, probably triggering our fellow worker to even more parental patterns: *I'll make you do it*, transmuted into "Well, I'll see it gets on your performance report!"

Most of us can recognize the dynamic. Often we deplore our own behavior and know we are complicating things when we respond that way, but we almost cannot help it. In some situations or relationships we just feel driven by those tapes. They take over. I have worked with some people who have just set me off. When they walk in the room, I'm ready to tell them why I won't do what they want me to, even before I know what they want. Then there are others I know are not going to do what I want, so in my anxiety I approach them very parentally.

Harris says that one of the few ways to break out of these unproductive exchanges is for someone to intervene with the "adult tape," which states facts or asks for data and tries to solve problems.[9] It attempts to focus attention on the issue at hand and it seeks collegiality in dealing with it. In the exchange I noted above about getting a report in on time, it might help if another fellow worker said, "Wait a minute. Who needs the report, and when do we have to have it ready? What do you need to get it done?" Harris says, and experience supports him, that just as a parent tape can trigger a child tape (and a child tape can trigger a parent tape) an adult tape can nudge people who are behaving parentally or childishly to get back into functional behavior.

What does all this have to do with churches and our need to transform them? Quite a bit.

The hierarchical structures that churches developed over the years have been overlaid by emotional interactions that closely fit the Harris model. The people, the offices, the structures at the "higher" levels often communicate with the "lower" levels using parent tapes. "You must do this, or we will report you to the annual conference. Get your contributions in on time. Where is your annual report?" Pastors relate to lay people too frequently out of their parent tapes: "Get to church on time. Not enough of you have increased your pledges. It is your responsibility to visit the sick."[10]

We should not be surprised by the childish responses: ignoring the messages; resenting the message and criticizing the messenger; dragging feet; being late; not carrying through on promises.

Then we compound the problem. We reward the congregations that do what they are asked, as if they were the "good children." They're the ones that don't get known around the judicatory office as being "problems" —the recalcitrant children you never can count on. On the congregational level, the obedient laypeople become the model leaders. The ones who ask difficult questions at parish meetings are soon seen as "troublemakers." Some congregations and some people become adolescent children who act out; they run away from denominational responsibility; they stay home and pout; they take their marbles and go home.

The connections I describe here are impressionistic, but they are real. Relationships in our organizational structures are overlaid by emotional baggage from past personal and organizational experience. Often congregations are responding emotionally to the way a bishop or a pastor or a national board acted years ago.

There is nothing "bad" in our acting this way. It is only bad if we do not recognize the patterns when we can and try to minimize unhelpful responses. It is bad only if our emotional baggage blocks us from examining the real issues we need to discuss and settle.

Specifically, we need to be aware of how pervasive these emotional triggers are, and we need to be alert to when we or our colleagues are moving into inappropriate behavior. We need to help one another relate as adult-to-adult so we can deal with what is really going on. As long as we are trapped in parental or childish tapes, we are being emotionally reactive to others; we are not making conscious choices or exploring what needs to be done.

There are structural things that can help. Elsewhere[11] I have pointed out that we need more accountability in our relationships in religious organizations. Pressing for clarity about expectations tends to move one toward adult relationships where what is to be done is thought through, defined, and spelled out. Parent-child agreements are often overlaid with unwritten expectations and undefined emotional contracts. Volunteers within a congregation need to get some clarity about what is expected of them and what resources they can count on to do their jobs. Otherwise they are pushed into the childish position of having to fantasize what is expected against the backdrop that one can never do enough. It is no wonder that volunteers burn out and grow resentful of how they have been treated.

The continuation of unhealthy forms of dependence is a barrier to the kinds of religious institutions we need. Being aware of this simple analysis of relational patterns may help us get out of emotional reactions when our parent tapes or our child tapes are triggered. And even if the awareness does not help us control our own reactions, the concept can be a resource to help us recognize these patterns in others.

We Have Become "Fundamentalists" in the Way We View our Structures[12]

In churches, perhaps more than any other place, we make idols out of our structures. We become fundamentalists about the forms by which we do what we do. We are fundamentalistic about what a pastor is, about how a congregation should be organized, about what a bishop or an executive is, about how one educates religious leaders. The *forms* become holy, and anyone who suggests changes in those structures is seen as a heretic.

I see parallel patterns in how we view the insides of the buildings we use for religious purposes. After a generation or two of use, the *furniture* takes on meaning. What was bought as a chair for the pastor to sit on when waiting to preach becomes *the pastor's chair*, and woe betide anyone who suggests that it be replaced.[13] Or even moved. Where it *is* becomes important. You can tell when the process is well along because things like pastors' chairs start having brass plaques attached and they become memorials to somebody. By then you are dead if you try to move it.

Different traditions have different areas of rigidity. Ask those in Catholic hierarchical roles about the authority of the priest or bishop, and you are likely to hear a response based on morphological fundamentalism, as this phenomenon has been called. Ask an Episcopalian why the laity should not celebrate the Eucharist, and you discover "the beast." Ask a Presbyterian why the presbytery executive cannot intervene in a clergy-lay congregational dispute, and you will see what I am talking about. Ask a United Methodist bishop about itinerancy or a Baptist or Congregationalist why their congregations cannot agree on a common policy....You get the picture.

Despite these differences, we share a terrible difficulty in being able to accept change in how we are structured, even when we become aware that the structures are not working well.[14] We are comfortable with the old ways. We've "grown accustomed to her face." That happens everywhere. Businesses and corporations have trouble changing things people have gotten used to. But religious institutions may have it more difficult than others.

Another paragraph about furniture may be instructive. When I got a new office chair, I felt a momentary pang. I loved the old one. Ted Eastman sold it to me eighteen years ago. My bottom was comfortable in it, and I knew which of the casters would fall off if you picked the chair up. But after one day in the new chair, which really did feel better and worked better, I lost my loyalty. But if you were to remove the bishop's chair from my parish church and replace it, I think I'd remember the old one Sunday after Sunday for years. They changed the altar rail (I really did not like the old one; it was dark; the brass fittings kept falling off; it threatened to collapse; and its color did not fit the other altar furniture), and after six months I still resent the new one.

Our current church structures are strangling us, but we love them. More than that, they feel holy to us. To change them *feels* like disloyalty to God—even though we know it's just a chair, just an organizational arrangement, just a leadership position.

We Have Not Recognized the Complexity of the Change Process

I trust we agree: We must renew our churches for the future. In doing so, perhaps our most difficult obstacle is our very complex relationship to change itself. Here I want to describe one strategic framework for approaching change and two ways of understanding reactions that block many change efforts. But I want to begin by putting the issue of change into perspective.

My Perspective on Change

Frankly, when it comes to change, I'd rather not deal with it. But I have to. The world I live in simply will not sit still. To maintain some kind of equilibrium and have some control over what's going on, I have to make fairly frequent adaptations if I want to stay in touch with my world.

If I were in a row boat in the middle of a lake, I could lie back and enjoy the sun and the motion of the ripples. Frankly, I'd like that...most of the time.

If, however, I were in a canoe in the middle of the rapids, my life would have to be very different. I would have to be alert for rocks under the surface. I would have to paddle to avert disaster or steer to safer water.

In the first scenario, I could go a long time not worrying about change—unless a storm came up. In the second, change is a matter of course. One kind of behavior works on the lake. The same behavior is disastrous if used in the rapids.

In today's world the churches are in the rapids. They are not the only ones. Actually, all our institutions are experiencing similar turbulence. Business corporations that try to maintain the practices that brought them to the top in the sixties or seventies see upstart companies cutting into their markets. Many such corporations will fall apart in the nineties. Some have begun to.

From my perspective, over the next few decades the religious structures that fail to change and learn to adapt will be like the buggy-whip manufacturers of the nineteenth century.

The changes needed in religious institutions may be even more urgent and fundamental than those needed in business. On the whole, businesses are required to maintain some flexibility to respond to their customers. But religious leaders have not been sensitive even to that organizational imperative. This neglect has put us in the position of having severe dislocations in the credibility and effectiveness of our institutions at the national, regional, and local levels. The further the ordinary lay member of the congregation is from an institutional structure, the more likely there will be a lack of credibility.

Let me be clear. I hold no brief for changing our basic message. I am a bit fundamentalistic at this point. I do not believe the basic message of the churches can or should change. But if our congregations are to be faithful to their revelation, they have to work regularly at how that unchanging truth needs to be presented in a changing time. They need to work at rethinking the structures and patterns that preserved those truths in the past to see what structures and patterns can do the same in our time.

In the language of my tradition, I do not believe the gospel itself changes. But to be faithful to that unchanging gospel in a changing world, I have to pay a lot of attention to (1) what is changing around me and (2) how I need to adapt in response. Religious leaders who agree with me on this point must be sure of two things: (1) that they are seen to be proclaimers of the gospel, not of change; and (2) that they keep their focus on that gospel; there is no other way to distinguish between that which can and should be changed and that which bears the stamp of the truth. In less elegant language, if you are bathing a baby it helps to be very clear about who the baby is when you need to throw out the bath water!

Although I refer here to the organizational necessity of dealing with change, my perspective is grounded much more deeply in what I understand to be God's will and God's call. I believe that the turmoil around us is at least partly God's invitation to us to join in the New Creation. Indeed, I understand what is going on as a working out of God's hope. As such, we are involved, as we deal with change, with eschatology. I sometimes describe my work with congregations and church bodies as "operational eschatology."

A Strategic Approach to Change

One of the multipurpose theories of change I have used over the years is
the simple and universally applicable framework laid down by behavioral scientist Kurt Lewin.[15] Lewin suggests that organizations are
rarely, if ever, at a point of total consensus about what they are and how
they should operate. Instead, organizations are in a state of organized
compromise, where the forces for change and the forces against change
are in equilibrium. This equilibrium is dynamic, not stable. Within a
certain range, the whole system can adapt to minor shifts and changes.
But there is a sense of mutual—often unspoken—agreement that the
equilibrium will not be changed in a basic way. (Although everyone in
the congregation knows that the order of the service is likely to have
some changes from time to time, everybody *knows* you better not mess
with the eleven o'clock hour!) That unspoken agreement is a powerful
force to keep change within limits. It makes for the status quo being a
kind of homeostasis. If changes are introduced that violate that unspoken
agreement, after a period of time things will probably revert to the
original homeostasis.

Here is a diagram of a system in homeostasis:

Over time this status quo becomes comfortable, and the different concerns are accommodated fairly well. The wide margins of the homeostatic system indicate some space for making adjustments in one direction or another without triggering anxious responses. Neither the people who push for change nor those who oppose it get all they want, but they have enough; and the system rests.

This understanding of an organization's equilibrium led Lewin to identify three stages one must go through to bring change into an organization. One must "unfreeze" the equilibrium. Then one must install the change (with all the adaptations of practice and training of organizational members). Then one must "refreeze" into a new homeostasis that includes the change.

Most attempts to install planned change in religious systems fail because the old systems are never unfrozen. A denomination or a judicatory will announce a great new idea or program that is bound to make a big difference. The announced program is then implemented to unanimous lack of enthusiasm by congregations that already have enough on their plates and want another new program the way they want a new mortgage. Year after year this goes on to the increasing frustration of the program designers—most of whom are pretty good at design. The homeostasis never gets broken open.[16]

The process of installing a change is generally done with little respect for the preexisting homeostasis—a homeostasis that includes a healthy respect for compromise. Most religious institutions install changes by strong advocacy of a particular point by the people who have power and want that change installed.

The homeostasis is upset by a strong intervention—often by the new pastor—pushing the system in the desired direction. Here is what generally happens when change is introduced this way:

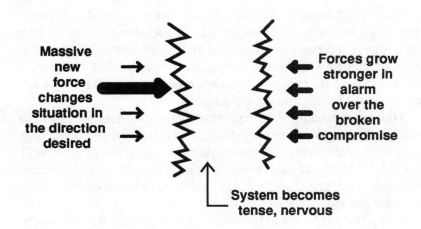

Yes, there is change. The strong input pushes the system in the desired direction. But look at the unintended by-products of this kind of change effort. First, those opposed to the change are startled and wake up to the fact that the truce has been broken. Their energy multiplies as they defend their territory, requiring greater and greater pressure from the pastor or another new intervener just to keep things in place. Not infrequently some of the people on the "change" side desert the ship; they do not want to get involved in a war! The change agent is more and more alone, working harder and harder to keep the gains made in the first push. But there is more. Look at the boundaries of the system. They have become constricted. The room for maneuvering and easy compromise is gone. Probably anything that gets proposed now will be the subject of suspicious nit-picking. Trust has been disrupted and opposition to change mobilized. The late stages of such a change effort are rarely comfortable. Indeed, when the pastor finally gives up or has a heart attack from the pressure, the homeostasis will probably be reestablished pretty much where it was before, except that trust levels will be lower when the next pastor arrives.

Lewin suggests that there is a better way to consider change, a way that is less confrontative and more collaborative and gives more promise of developing sustainable change without loss of trust. Here is a diagram of his suggestion:

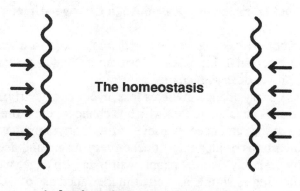

1. Analyze forces on *both* sides.

2. Develop strategies on *both* sides to maintain trust and to effect change using already present energy.

Lewin encourages change agents instead to do careful diagnosis of the equilibrium, identifying proponents of change and opponents to change, analyzing the forces involved. Both sides of the homeostasis are included in the planning and thinking about what is needed. By doing so the effort is broadened, and the legitimate concerns of potential opponents to the change are brought into the conversation early enough to make significant impact on what is actually planned. The entire system, not just those hell-bent for a change, works on plans and strategies. Those who use this approach (it is called "force field analysis") find that the resulting change efforts have a high survival rate. The trust in the system can actually expand when this is done well. And the new homeostasis has a chance of being as stable as the last.

What Lewin calls refreezing is universally ignored in change efforts in religious institutions. The institutions act as if once a change is set in place, opposition no longer exists. Refreezing a changed system involves training people in the behaviors needed, making periodic evaluations to take into account what has gone wrong, and listening to opposition, ever seeking to improve the quality of the new homeostasis. Again, collaborative planning and strategizing are helpful, making for a healthier aftermath to change.

The Personal Dimension of Response to Change--Grief

Elisabeth Kubler-Ross's book *On Death and Dying*[17] is a wonderful guide to how personal responses to loss can influence a person's or a group's ability to deal with change.

Because every change involves loss, every change triggers grief. The more one is attached to that which is changed, the more intense one's sense of loss and need to grieve. Almost anything that touches religious memories or meanings touches very strong and deep feeling. That is why perfectly rational people will roar with anger when someone moves something as simple as a chair in the sanctuary of a church. That is why strong, able people can become frantic and panic-stricken when they hear that their pastor has been called to another job—even people who did not particularly like the pastor. It is as if the religious factor acts as a magnifying glass for losses. The responses are often multiplied out of proportion to "reality."

Kubler-Ross notes several characteristic responses to loss—denial, bargaining, anger/guilt, depression, acceptance. Individual responses are not sequential and may recur in cycles. Having reached some level of acceptance of a loss, one may still revert to seasons of anger or depression. She teaches us that grieving takes time; in time one can move beyond the grief.

Religious leaders who deal in change need to be aware of the need to minister to all those responses. Change, and responding to it, must be understood to be very time-consuming and deeply emotional. Change is not simply "fixing something." It requires real pastoral care and spiritual discernment.

Pastors often see their work so exclusively as managing the change process that they do not recognize how critical it is to minister to the spiritual needs that block people from being able to accept change. Actually, there is more than enough change—and grief—in anyone's life *even if the pastor institutes no changes whatsoever*.

If I note a characteristic fault of religious leaders it is that they respond to the symptom and consequently miss the opportunity to deal with the larger religious issue—whether it be the fear of the unknown, the threat of death, or the question of ultimate meaning. Religious leaders respond as if the expressed anger or depression were the issue, when the issues are deeper.

Also, many pastors worry about this or that angry parishioner, the poor, depressed people who have given up on life, or the "church rats" who are constantly underfoot, trying to do anything and everything to please the pastor. They overlook the needs of the grim-faced stoic who avoids thinking about change by becoming the rock-ribbed bulwark of the status quo. Pastors I know see these characteristic types in terms of how they affect the congregation's program, not in terms of their substantial spiritual need as they face the loss of familiar and valued parts of their lives.

Pastors and church leaders who understand the changes needed in their systems and have worked hard to get them installed have done less than half the job. The more important part is the religious, pastoral, and spiritual task of nurturing, pushing, and supporting people as they see their world change. In the long run, one of the most important functions of a religious organization is as a laboratory in which people are given an opportunity to discover God in the process of living with change and loss. Too tight a focus on the change itself short-circuits that deeper pastoral task.

Many church members carry substantial loads of unresolved grief. It comes from a variety of places—disappointments over lost opportunities, remembrances of lost loved ones, bitterness about real or imagined unfairness, alienation or a sense of having been left out or left behind. Everyone has a personal version of this sense of loss, and everyone carries it alongside his or her personal strengths and weaknesses. Similarly, as a society we bear a sense of loss as a people—loss of the memory of a kinder, gentler nation than we see today, loss of our dreams of what the nation might become, loss of certain hopes.

In that context, what goes on in congregations as we learn to deal with change is, in fact, a doorway for Grace to enter into hidden griefs in personal lives, touching those unhealed places each of us has. Dealing with change and the emotions it raises in our congregations can potentially connect us (as healing conduits) to the pain and grief that wracks our society.

Understanding change as opportunity for spiritual ministry in this way—depth ministry to individual memory and life, and breadth ministry to society's pain—should put a new dimension on the hassles of moving church furniture, winning or losing parish elections, and approaching difficult planning issues.

Organizational Dimensions of Change--Shock and Adaptation

Another important theory about the organizational dimension of change gives us clues to what is going on in religious institutions and may suggest directions for the future.

Writing in a recessionary time some years ago, Fink, Beak, and Taddeo[18] described how organizations they worked with faced crises. The response pattern they discovered in those organizations is congruent with what Kubler-Ross discovered in people--with one difference. Kubler-Ross said that the emotional responses she found in those facing death did not follow a clear sequence. One stage did not lead to the next in a sequential or fully predictable way. Fink, Beak, and Taddeo seem to suggest that the four stages of the response pattern they identified in organizations follow one another sequentially. The organizations that do not move on from one stage to the next may simply not survive to tell the story. Organizations may not have adequate identity to recycle through stages that have not been completed.

Fink, Beak, and Taddeo describe four sequential stages for the organizations that surmount crises: shock, defensive retreat, acknowledgment, and growth and adaptation.

In most organizations shock is the immediate response to crisis. Many of the people in the organization share a visceral understanding that something is seriously wrong. During shock the organization's members fragment, and almost everyone moves into a stance of taking care of himself, distancing self from others. People or groups are blamed, and anger is bitter, often focused on specific actors in the drama. Communications get muddled and trust disappears. Fights break out among groups and individuals. No one has energy to think about the future. If the leaders panic along with everyone else, the others can be particularly demoralized. One of the hopeful organizational dynamics is that different groups hit shock at different times. For example, if the leaders see the crisis early enough and deal with their own shock, they are better able to help when shock hits the troops! Throughout the process, it is best if leaders can deal with their own issues early and mobilize other levels of their group to move on to the next stage.

Defensive retreat is a difficult stage. It is marked by imposition of tight controls, a "clamping down." Budgets may be slashed. People get fired.[19] Although this period rarely solves any basic problems, it can keep the group from total disintegration. Sometimes the budget cuts and staff terminations bring costs temporarily under control and preserve enough financial viability to allow the company to survive. But a prolonged period of shock and denial may have led to such a depletion of financial reserves that even this short-term strategy is too late. The better the leaders have been in processing their own shock, the more likely they will be able to hold things together. When defensive retreat hits the organization's leaders, many others may be experiencing the initial shock of hearing "the news." This is not a time that really faces the future; at this point the survivors begin to find new patterns of working together. You can expect an "in group" and an "out group" with continuing suspicion between them. Flow of information is often rigidly controlled. Anything the organization started right before the crisis—a new program, a new management system, a new bookkeeping system—may be the first thing thrown out, even though it has much promise. The group may revert to previous behavior and previous structures. Leaders are tempted to demand loyalty to the system and to impose authoritarian leadership styles.

Fink, Beak, and Taddeo say that acknowledgment comes to many who survive shock and defensive retreat. (Some do not survive either.)

This marks a turn toward the future. Acknowledgment represents the organization's turning the corner from anger and blame to a search for answers. Here we try to find out what we must not do. Instead of "who's to blame?" the question is "what went wrong?" and it is asked to figure out how to avoid the same mistakes in the future. Acknowledgment often includes a new look at the environment and the organization's "customers" to determine what signals had been missed. This stage questions how things have been done in the past and thinks about new paths. Leadership often relaxes a bit from its tight need to control everything and everybody. Personal relationships among colleagues become less anxious and suspicious. People begin to want to work together on common tasks.

Institutions that make it through the acknowledgment stage can move into the fourth stage—*growth and adaptation.* This is when the organization's coping mechanisms kick back in. The focus is the future, not the past. The purposes and vision of the organization are reexamined and people set out to build for the future. Often new myths build up about "the time we nearly went under."

These theories, based in business organizations, are not totally de-scriptive of what goes on in religious organizations facing crisis. But I see many parallels. My own diagnosis is that most of the national struc-tures of the mainline churches are in shock, with a few giving signs of having moved to defensive retreat. Of the more conservative Protestant churches and the Roman Catholic Church, I see signs of some people and groups moving into shock, but overall little response to the environmen-tal changes around them.

In the mainline churches, a prolonged shock and denial stage among leaders has seriously eroded the financial base for moving ahead into defensive retreat. Regional structures of the churches seem even more threatened, but all too few leaders at that level have begun to face the crisis.

Conclusion

In earlier chapters I have noted the key tasks congregations must address to fulfill their purpose and the functions congregations need from de-nominational systems if they are to fulfill that purpose in the midst of the serious storm we face. Of course responding to these challenges will set churches on a new course of rethinking and reconstructing things that are very basic to their lives.

In this chapter I have laid out the more difficult organizational issues that block our moving ahead. Right now we can begin to address any one—or all—of these obstacles, and I have given some clues as to how and where to start.

I wrap this section up with one final sobering challenge: The ques-tion of reinventing the church—on our side—may come down to *will*.

CHAPTER 6

Transformation and Congregations

Twenty-five hundred years ago Jerusalem was laid waste by an enemy from Babylon. The conquerors destroyed the city that had nurtured rebellion and resistance once too many times. The temple that dated back to David's son was destroyed, with the stones of its foundation left like the ruins of Coventry Cathedral after the Second World War. The gates of the great city of Jerusalem were pulled down as were the walls that had protected the citizens. A great dream of a nation held together as a political state within a framework of religious vocation seemed to be gone forever.

Jeremiah lived as a community leader and a prophet during the last days before that city fell. At times viewed as a national wise man and hero, at other times vilified as a traitor and fool, Jeremiah read the signs of the times against his understanding of God's will, and he called for repentance and change. As the people continued in a suicidal course, Jeremiah read their fate and spoke of the inevitable destruction to come.

Then, with the enemy at the gate, with the destruction he had foreseen immediately present, Jeremiah changed his message and course of action, this also based on this faith and his understanding of God. As everyone else looked at destruction, Jeremiah announced that God would bring new life to the city and to the fields that surrounded it. He predicted that the vineyards and orchards would again be fruitful and that the city would flourish.

With his known world obviously coming to an end, Jeremiah purchased a field in the village of Anathoth as a demonstration of his confidence in the future and in God's promises.

We can understand Jeremiah's time. Although there is no army currently at the gate, much of our civilization seems to be under threat, if not actually in collapse. Our society, like Jeremiah's, is emerging from a sense of religious and political unity and clarity into a cacophony of voices and powers. Called to serve God's world, we have lost the clarity of our vocation and of our direction. The structures of our society and faith have failed to keep us focused on that vocation of service, and often those structures of service and mission have become self-serving. Rather than being servants of God's purposes in the world, we have too often become servants of the structures themselves.

My first message about transforming congregations is that we must do as Jeremiah did: In spite of the wisdom of the world, we are called to commit ourselves unreservedly to the future of God's promises. In Jeremiah's case, that commitment took the prosaic form of making an investment in real estate. In our time, it may be just as prosaic. We are the generation whose gift to the future may not be a complete vision of the new society or even the new church, but the example of holding steady and faithful as the landmarks of the world we have known disintegrate. Our task is to go on holding on, studying and teaching the story of the faith, acting in service to the world, trusting God in the middle of ambiguity, refusing to back away from God's claim upon us. If we hold steady, God will provide the vision when the time is right.

As for the new society and the new church, we will see only the beginnings of transformation. Jeremiah's actions spoke then to his contemporaries, and they have spoken to people of faith for these twenty-five hundred years. He may have bought that field as a specific witness to us. A king named Cyrus was to open the door for the return to Jerusalem. Jeremiah bought the field long before Cyrus was born. Jeremiah died long before that field had its first crop.

The first step in transformation has to do with attitude. (We'll get to tasks in a minute.) We need a simple commitment to the future, obedience to God's promise. There is a difference between the commitment I propose and what the churches seem to be doing. Jeremiah's commitment was not a denial of the destruction of Jerusalem and the exile of the people. Our commitment must be large enough to acknowledge the winds of the storm we are in and go through the storm, not pretend it is unreal. The life of God's people was fundamentally reshaped by the years in exile. As we move into a historical arena in which the church is no longer the center, in which Christendom and Crusades are terms of the past, we have new pages to write about what church is and how we can serve. We will know it only by going ahead.

Two or three generations after the fall of Jerusalem, the exiles in Babylon were startled to learn that a new king had opened the door for them to return to rebuild their beloved city and their temple. The book of Ezra, Nehemiah, Haggai, and Zechariah preserve some of the story of that time and the flavor of a people struggling to rebuild a nation.

The story can be instructive to us, particularly if their task is analogous to that which we face in our time. Perhaps the clearest message is that not everyone in that day was enthusiastic about the task of transformation. Historical records suggest that the first exiles to return with enthusiasm to restore the kingdom and the temple waited nearly twenty years before they started to build. In the press of other things—getting crops planted and harvested, getting families started, worrying about trade and defense—they forgot what they went back to do.

The faith reasons for returning home took back seat to the details of making a living. And even that did not work. Their crops failed, their vineyards did not produce. The people grumbled and fought as they lost direction.

The prophetic voices of Haggai and Zechariah called the people back to their real task of faithfulness. Two tasks were laid out and, in time, accomplished: The city's walls were rebuilt with its gates restored, and in the center of the city a new temple was raised up from the ruins of the old.

Those two tasks are central for us today: rebuilding the city wall and restoring the temple.

Rebuilding the Wall

The first *task* in our transformation is the rebuilding of the city wall. The city wall of Jerusalem distinguished what was inside the city from what was outside. It helped the city establish its identity. So for us in our congregational life. We must clarify what makes us different, so that we can undertake our vocation as apostles. This requries us to establish the authenticity and distinctiveness of our congregations so that we live visibly in our faith, shaped by the biblical heritage, not by the least common denominator of local values and morality. We must build congregations where people know and follow Jesus, not the latest polls.

Those congregations must become centers that can provide space for genuine encounter, where one may be confronted and supported in the deep experiences of life. These congregations must be communities that can help each of us discover our gifts and our special vocation to serve our society. Rebuilding the wall means clarifying the boundary of the community and continuing to maintain it. It involves getting clearer and clearer about what is inside and what is not inside the community. In our tradition it means actively welcoming those who come to the congregation, but carefully training them in the stories of the faith.

Within our traditon, the wall, the boundary, is not for the purpose of separation but of service. The function of the boundary is not to exclude but to help the community strengthen its identity and its commitment to serving. The purpose of the community is to increase its ability for each to reach out beyond the boundary. The integrity of the wall is to help the community in its continuing effort to discern its mission and that of each member.

Congregations, following the example of those who returned from exile in Babylon, have first the task of rebuilding the city wall so that the people can once again grasp their identity in this alien and confusing world. The wall defines the community that is a training ground for disciples. It establishes the community that sends its members out in service and receives them back for healing and nurture. The wall is to help the community intensify its thrust out beyond the wall.

We are called to reestablish the boundary between our congregations and the society around them, getting clear about the cultural distance between followers of the values of this world and followers of the gospel. We are powerless to change ourselves and the world if we are confused about what our community stands for.

Restoring the Temple

The other task the exiles postponed but eventually took on was the restoration of the temple. One can sympathize. Surely it must have seemed more important to clear the stones from the fields and get the crops in before focusing on the temple. It was more important to get roofs over the heads of the children than to rebuild the altars and restore the worship.

The scripture-story indicates that the exiles were wrong. Common wisdom is wrong. It is not more important to do anything at all other than restore the temple. Our assumptions about what is "logical, prudent, and rational" are based on a set of values that are not the same as the values of our faith.

This may be the most difficult point for us, living as we do on the change-point of the centuries. We are so practical. We must see the usefulness of a course of action. We want to justify activities, actions, or programs by their "outcomes" and "productivity." These stories from the scriptures remind us that when dealing with the things of God, we are not dealing in our familiar world. The world of Jeremiah and Zechariah is a world in which two plus two may add up to *apple*, not just *four*. The world of faith makes strange leaps from one thing to another. Disciples criticize a woman for wasting expensive lotion on Jesus, and he rejects their social-action concerns. Temples are not very productive. I can understand why the exiles left that until the "real" work was done.

Too many of us are not comfortable with the suggestion that such priority be given to that which is "religious" as opposed to that which is "efficacious." Indeed, that very distinction is questionable. But the point is that *what the church is is more important than what it does*.

And the heart of the church's being is the deep conversation between God and God's people that the community works out in its life of worship—in its temple. That is why it is critical to restore the temple. And this comes first. It comes before improving our institutional framework; it comes before training our clergy; it comes before organizing programs for feeding the hungry or housing the homeless; it comes before establishing nonsexist, nonracist relationships.

The life of worship and prayer is absolutely first. It is not an optional extra. That is the difficult message from scripture for us. I think we need to allow that reality to confront us and challenge us and our rationalizations.

Every bone in our bodies yearns to recruit new members, raise more money, revise our rules of order, and learn how to market our church as well as others market theirs. We want to develop better education programs. We want our judicatory to restructure itself. We want to do some really basic long-term planning. Strategic planning. I do not downplay the importance of these many ministries we have developed over time. Nothing I say takes away from the fact that people are often called to reach out in response to urgencies that demand their response.

But those who care for religious institutions need to square up to the fact that restoring the temple is top priority.

Conclusion

Churches I have known for more than six decades and served professionally for nearly four are in a serious storm. The storm is most obvious in the collapsing structures of some of them—the ones we ironically have called mainline. If I am right, those signs of stress and strain are only symptoms of the larger storm that will engulf people of faith in many other religious families in the next decades. The churches we have known have been nurtured at the heart of our society. In our time we are moving into an exile from the heart of our society. I believe the movement is irreversible. The triumphalism of the conservative churches today becomes them no better than did the similar attitude of the mainline churches in the fifties. I doubt that the triumphalism will last much longer for the one than for the other.

My concern is to seek to help congregations of any kind—conservative, liberal, or what have you—reclaim the essential task of making disciples, one by one, and launching each of them as an apostle into the society he or she faces, wherever it is and whatever it may be like.

To do that, congregations need to transform their inner life so that their community reflects the *koinonia* of the early church's congregations. They need a sense of community that transforms the lives of members. They need to develop a ministry of *kerygma* where the story of the people of God comes alive in the power of the Spirit through the proclamation of the gospel. They need to develop a ministry of teaching, *didache*, that presents the age-old story fresh to new generations and with transforming power to those called to be apostles. They need new power to understand and reflect on their serving in the world, their *diakonia*.

That looks inside congregations, to the transformations we must make in them so that they may transform us into disciples. But the end of becoming a disciple is to be transformed into an apostle. Discipleship is the passive, but necessary grounding for the life of faith. Apostleship is the active voice for faithful living.

I want every congregation feeding apostles into the towns and cities, the agencies and the structures, the families and the neighborhoods of our society. I want every member of every congregation to know him- or herself to be called to a servant ministry, the apostolate, and I want each to have help discerning his or her gifts and to be trained and nurtured in his or her vocation. That calls for congregations that can transform ordinary people into apostles. I look for each congregation to be that kind of a transforming congregation.

For that to happen, I want to see the structures that surround congregations—the judicatories, the national structures, the seminaries, and educational institutions—building skills in new ways, ready to help transform congregations from what they are to what they must be as centers of apostolic ministry. I want all those structures working at transforming congregations.

There are more roadblocks than I have listed in chapter 5. And each impediment is formidable. There are some things we can do to dismantle the roadblocks, things I have described in this book, and things that others are working on and learning about. But transformation occurs one person, one congregation, at a time, uniquely.

There is great good news in that fact. Every congregation is on the front edge of possibility and can begin its work of transformation. There is not a special kind of congregation or people that has the answer. This is not a task cut out for only the big congregations with high steeples and large staffs. This is not an invitation only to Baptist or to Episcopal or to independent congregations. The call is open to each and the opportunity for discovery is there for each. Each is called to start where it is.

Each congregation can begin now to commit itself to following God's purposes, come what may—bigger budgets or smaller ones, more members or fewer. Each can make a commitment to sending apostles in service to its world. Now.

The future is genuinely open. None of us has all the wisdom or the resources we need to rebuild our churches. But all of us have enough to start. In the end, I can summarize what I know into two statements:

— The time is right for us to make the commitment Jeremiah made—a commitment against all reason to the future and to God's promises.
— The tasks before us are the tasks that faced the exiles returning to Jerusalem—to rebuild the walls of the city and to restore the temple.

What lies ahead is a storm, indeed. The winds are strong, and we cannot know all that is to come. But in and through this storm, a transforming Power is at work to build an apostolic church. To be called to participate in that transformation is our life.

The Good-News/Bad-News Quadrilateral: A Design

Introduction

The following design is based on an educational model I have used in many different situations. It helps people get in touch with the many ways people and groups conceive of their special call to serve. I find it helps people understand the diversity of their congregation; it legitimizes different responses to the gospel; it helps people get an overall sense of the ministry of their group; and it raises helpful questions about the function of the larger group in relationship to the ministry of the individual. My experience with this design and comments of hundreds with whom I have used it lie beneath much of what I say in chapters 2 and 3.

The Basic Theory

I see evangelism not as a "program" or organized activity but as a basic human response to God's continuous vocation to each human being. I see that continuous vocation to be almost like a gravitational pull to each of us to respond as cocreators of God's kingdom. The more conscious we are of God's grace in our own lives, the more conscious and intentional we may be in responding. On the other hand, whether or not we are conscious of the call in any rational way, we may still be pulled into response at a level deeper than our minds. Those of us with the gift of articulation can name the good news. But many of us proclaim the good news without using words of explanation. We may not even understand why we are impelled to act, and some who are evangelists may not even know in whose Name we perceive bad news and in whose Name the good news flows. Where it is God's will, the action of witnessing to the good news elicits the response of the one leper who returned to Jesus from among the ten who were cleansed. I always hope that "the ten" will return, but remember that for Jesus one was enough.

I see evangelism as profoundly situational. I see it as profoundly individual. I see it as being generated within each of us as God opens our eyes and sensitivity to the hurts of the world around us. I see the focus of each person's evangelism as shifting from time to time, driven by inner sensitivities, a sense of Grace, and the leading of God. I see our congregations as the places where our sensitivities are nourished and our evangelism fed, primarily by Word and Sacrament, but also by the community itself (*koinonia*) and the teaching (*didache*).

This design invites people to read their own evangelistic location within a map of evangelistic possibility. It helps them reflect upon that location in relationship to the location of others in the group and to the overall picture of the strengths and weaknesses they perceive in their community's openness to need.

The Process of the Design

Step 1: Introduce the activity with a brief bit of theory, generally a description of the important link between good news and bad news, as described in chapter 2. The examples of Martin Luther King, Jr. and Billy Graham help people connect the idea with their experience.

Step 2: Cautions. I invite people into the exercise as an experiment in perception, noting that it is not a scientific study. I particularly press the point that I am asking them to respond in terms of where they are today, at this moment. I note that yesterday and tomorrow they may well be in different places. I visualize it as a still photograph from a moving picture.

Step 3: Two forced-choice questions. I invite—no, I push, press—everyone to make one choice for each of two continua. I urge all to be simplistic, to indicate just where they see themselves as being at this moment, ignoring complexities. Then I give them the first "command":

The continuum ranges from number 1 to number 10. I will describe number 1 and I will describe number 10. If what I describe is exactly where you are right now, then write a 1 or a 10. Probably you are somewhere between, so just guess. If you're close to 1, maybe you are at 2 or 3; if you're close to 10, maybe you're at 7 or 8. Just make a choice. Place yourself on a line between these two statements:

Number 1:   The *only* way to know God is in a one-on-one, direct relationship. That's the *only* way to know God.

Number 10:   The *only* way to know God is in the midst of God's people, the church. That's the *only* way.

After a minute or two, during which I quell the grumbling and push them to go on and make a choice, I give them the second continuum. By now they know the ropes, so you don't have to give as much explanation. This time I make the choice in terms of the alphabet, and the choice ranges from A to J. I describe A and I describe J, and they choose their position in relationship to the extremes.

Letter A: The end and purpose of life is so to live that I am reunited with God at my death.

Letter J: The end and purpose of life is to participate with brothers and sisters in building a human society of shalom, where peace and justice and love reign.

Step 4: If I am working with newsprint, I draw a graph with the two continua as the axes. (A copy of the graph is appended, suitable for copying onto an overhead transparency if you prefer that method.) Then I call on members of the group to call out their own coordinates. As they do so, I make a mark at the appropriate spot on the map. The faster, the better. (If you have a conspicuous religious leader *of this group* present, I usually ask that pastor or bishop or president *not* to call out his or her coordinates. This is so that people will not stereotype their leader.)

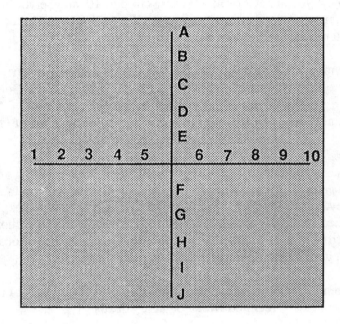

Step 5: Reflection and plenary discussion. Some of the areas in which I invite discussion:

1. The variety of responses. *All* points on the grid are legitimate positions, positions that have been held by great saints.

2. Reflect on where "clumps" of people show up. What does that mean?

3. Reflect on where there is a dearth of responses. What does that mean?

4. What does the overall pattern say about possible strengths of this particular group in ministry? What things are they most likely to be aware of? Most likely to care about?

5. What does the pattern say about the blind spots of this group?

6. I invite people to respond to how their personal choices felt. I particularly invite those whose coordinates were "far out" from the center, or in a quadrant with few or no others, how it felt to call out their locations. (You can sometimes help the group understand the emotional pressure we exert on one another to conform.)

Step 6: Interpretation. I summarize what the group has learned in the exercise. I sometimes use more material from chapter 2, the descriptions of the quadrants, for example. I usually refer the group to the similar typologies developed by Roozen, McKinney, and Carroll. My major concern at this point is to help them think of the *function* of the pastor and of the congregation *not* to bring the congregation's "center" to where the pastor wants it or to where the majority "clump" of the congregation wants it, but to "hold the center," nourishing and feeding all the diverse ministries. I try to help them identify "lacks" in their congregation or consciousness that, if added, might increase the overall strength of the ministry. The stronger the center, in my opinion, the greater the extremes that can be supported.

Step 7: Wild applause.

APPENDIX B

The Statistics Behind the Graphs

The graphs of the memberships of the Epicsopal Church, the Presbyterian Church, the United Church of Christ, the United Methodist Church, and the Evangelical Lutheran Church in America were based on data from Table A1.1 of the Appendix of *Church and Denominational Growth,* edited by David A. Roozen and C. Kirk Hadaway (Nashville, Abingdon, 1994). The graphs plotting the U.S. population were based on figures reported on page 361 of *The World Almanac and Book of Facts: 1994* (Mahwah, NJ: World Almanac Books, 1993).

The specific numbers used are listed on the following page.

Population of the United States

1950	151,325,798
1960	179,323,175
1970	203,302,031
1980	226,542,203
1990	248,709,873

Membership by Denomination

	Episcopalian	Presbyterian	UCC	UMC	ELCA
1950	2,417,464	3,210,635	1,977,428	9,653,178	3,982,508
1960	3,269,325	4,161,860	2,241,134	10,641,310	5,295,502
1970	3,285,826	4,045,408	1,960,608	10,509,198	5,650,137
1980	2,786,004	3,362,086	1,736,244	9,519,407	5,384,271
1990	2,446,050	2,847,437	1,599,212	8,904,824	5,240,739

Denominational Membership
as a Percentage of U.S. Population

	Episcopalian	Presbyterian	UCC	UMC	ELCA
1950	1.60%	2.12%	1.31%	6.38%	2.63%
1960	1.82%	2.32%	1.25%	5.93%	2.95%
1970	1.62%	1.99%	.96%	5.17%	2.78%
1980	1.23%	1.48%	.77%	4.20%	2.38%
1990	.98%	1.14%	.64%	3.58%	2.11%

Introduction

1. Loren B. Mead, *The Once and Future Church* (Washington, DC: The Alban Institute, 1991).

2. Loren B. Mead, *More Than Numbers* (Washington, DC: The Alban Institute, 1993).

3. Loren . Mead, "Operational Theology" in *Patterns in Parish Development*, ed. Celia Allison Hahn (New York: Seabury Press, 1974), pp. 157-58.

Chapter 1

1. C. Kirk Hadaway, *What Can We Do About Church Dropouts?* (Nashville: Abingdon Press, 1990), ch. 2-3.

2. Kenneth B. Bedell, ed., *Yearbook of American and Canadian Churches* (Nashville: Abingdon Press, 1993). The data for the illustrations also draws on the figures from many such annual reports as published in David A. Roozen and C. Kirk Hadaway, ed., *Church and Denominational Growth* (Nashville: Abingdon Press, 1993), appen., Table A1.1. This raw data is noted in Appendix B. In the interests of accuracy it must be noted that in several years since 1990 the Episcopal Church has showed a small net gain in numbers, but not percent of population. This encouraging statistic is, however, problematic in that the definition of "member" was slightly changed.

3. Figures 1, 3, and 5 chart denominations categorized as "liberal Protestant." Figures 2 and 4 are for denominations categorized as "moderate Protestant." Any such designations involve difficult judgment

calls. These categories are described in William McKinney and W. Clark Roof, *Mainline American Religion* (New York: Pilgrim Press, 1984). The same categories are used in Roozen and Hadaway, *Church and Denominational Growth.*

4. Fellow North Carolinians may remember a classic story about how things have changed in churches when it comes to pointing fingers in blame. Bunny Boyd was an immensely popular professor of religion at the University of North Carolina in the forties and fifties, when the Revised Standard Version was first released. In backwoods Carolina the newfangled language for the familiar stories was a shock, to say the least. One conservative pastor staged a book burning at Rocky Mount. This hit the headlines in newspapers across the state and caused an uproar in Professor Boyd's nine o'clock class. "What about what happened in Rocky Mount?" they asked.

"What happened?" he responded, not having checked the morning's News and Disturber.

They told him about the book burning and he replied, "Wonderful!"

When asked to defend his statement, he said, "Book burning is much better. We used to burn the people who translated it!"

5. Dean R. Hoge and David A. Roozen, ed., *Understanding Church Growth and Decline* (New York: Pilgrim Press, 1979). See especially ch. 14, "Some Sociological Conclusions about Church Trends," 315-33. See also Andrew Greeley, *Religious Change in America* (Cambridge, Mass.: Harvard University Press, 1989).

6. Dean R. Hoge, Benton Johnson, and Donald Luidens, *Vanishing Boundaries The Religion of Mainline Baby Boomers* (Louisville: Westminster/John Knox, 1994). Findings are summarized in a number of papers and articles, including "What Happened to the Youth Who Grew Up in Our Churches," *Congregations*, no. 5 (September-October 1992).

7. In fairness to the authors, I need to say that this is not their main point. They are doing an impressive study of what has happened to baby boomers in one denomination. Even this minor point of theirs is an extremely important new issue for denominational leaders to take into account. How much more impressive is the rest of the book.

8. See Roozen and Hadaway, *Church and Denominational Growth.*

9. Data in these two graphs are derived from data noted in Appendix B. The idea of the graphs is dervied from *Vanishing Boundaries.*

Two things show dramatically here: the period of anomalous growth between about 1945 and 1965 and the steeper downward slope of recent church membership.

10. Here Hoge, Johnson, and Luidens, *Vanishing Boundaries*, makes its major contributions. See also McKinney and Roof, *Mainline American Religion*.

11. I tell my denominational friends that our budget reductions remind me of a Carolina friend who had a marvelous hunting dog that he took hunting every Saturday. Trouble was, the dog's tail was long and shaggy, and it would pick up cockleburs. By Monday he would have chewed them all out, but he also had a mass of painful sores. Yet the dog loved to hunt. . . . So the owner said, "The only thing I can think to do is to make him a bob-tailed dog." He continued, "But I really don't want to hurt him. So I think I'll just cut off an inch of tail at a time!" I rest my case.

12. *Church Membership Statistics: 1970-1980* (Washington, DC: The Alban Institute, 1983).

13. Gay Jennings, unpublished report, Episcopal Diocese of Ohio, 2230 Euclid Ave., Cleveland, OH 44115. Some similar points are made in Dean Hoge, Jackson W. Carroll, and Francis K. Scheets, *Patterns of Parish Leadership* (Kansas City, Mo.: Sheed and Ward, 1988). This book examines the cost of providing professional leadership in congregations of four denominations: Episcopal, Roman Catholic, Evangelical Lutheran Church in America, and United Methodist. The research was carried out on 1984 budgets, so it dealt with one of the Lutheran bodies that later formed the Evangelical Lutheran Church in America.

14. Hoge, Johnson, and Luidens, "What Happened to the Youth Who Grew Up in Our Churches," *Congregations*.

Chapter 2

1. Loren B. Mead, *The Once and Future Church* (Washington, DC: The Alban Institute, 1991), 20-22.

2. It is interesting to note that some of Jesus' ways of proclaiming the gospel are no longer open to us because other of his followers beat us to it. Jesus healed many lepers in his day, and those who follow him have come close to eliminating leprosy around the world.

3. The truth is probably much more complex than I have stated here. See David Roozen, William McKinney, and Jackson Carroll, *Varieties of Religious Presence* (New York: Pilgrim Press, 1984), a provocative book based on important studies of churches in the Hartford, Connecticut area. It describes four types of congregations in terms of how each understands its relationship to its environment. Their four categories of group identities are quite close to the quadrants I have noted here for individual relationship to the world: quadrant A being analogous to their "sanctuary church"; quadrant B corresponding to "evangelistic church"; quadrant C to "civic church"; and quadrant D to "activist church." Carl Dudley's research in the Midwest suggests an even more complex set of categories than these. One wonders about the possibility that congregations may, in their own cultures, preserve important and different sensitivities to good news. This may be an unexplored frontier for thinkers about ecumenism.

Chapter 3

1. I once saw this prophetic message acted out. I was in Washington at the time of Helen Keller's death, and I attended her funeral at the National Cathedral. The blind, the deaf, and the lame were there, celebrating her life. A choir from a school for the blind sang like angels. Sen. Lister Hill of Alabama read the lesson with a powerful voice trained in southern oratory. For the first time in my life I watched as the lesson was signed. As he spoke of the deaf hearing, the blind seeing, the lame leaping for joy, we saw the good news acted out even as we also experienced God's power in the life of Helen Keller.

2. Parker Palmer, *Going Public* (Washington, DC: The Alban Institute, 1980). This monograph is out of print but available as an on-demand publication from The Alban Institute, 4550 Montgomery Ave., Suite 433 N., Bethesda, MD 20814-3341.

3. Robert Bellah, et al., *Habits of the Heart* (Berkeley: University of California Press, 1985).

4. In 1972 Tilden Edwards, Parker Palmer, James Simmons, and I talked to a group of twenty laypeople about their experiences of spiritual growth. The paper we wrote, *Spiritual Growth*, is out of print (Project Test Pattern, 1973). Jean Haldane made similar discoveries, reported in

Religious Pilgrimage (Washington, DC: The Alban Institute, 1975). In more recent times Gallup polls have found among interviewees a high number of personal experiences with God.

5. Keith Russell argues that Koinonia *was* the primary thing the early church had to offer society. People were drawn to the church because its living community spoke to the bad news of their society. See *In Search of the Church* (Washington, DC: The Alban Institute, 1994).

6. As an Episcopalian myself, I am well aware that many of my non-Episcopal friends understand "Episcopal preacher" to be an oxymoron!

7. For more details see Loren B. Mead, *More Than Numbers* (Washington, DC: The Alban Institute, 1993), ch. 3.

8. For a fuller exploration of the theories, see Bruce Reed, *The Dynamics of Faith* (London: Darton, Longman, and Todd, 1978). For a shorter version, see Bruce Reed and Barry Palmer, *The Task of the Church and the Role of Its Members* (Washington, DC: The Alban Institute, 1975). Reed's work in group relations and the dynamics of organizations has been critically important to many in this country. I am particularly indebted to him.

9. I have never fully understood the fascination certain denominations have exhibited in the use of the New Testament role of the deacon as a special agent and representative of the church in the world (what I have characterized as the apostolate). My own understanding is that the baptized person operating as an apostle is the church's representative to the world.

10. The placements I note here are the sort that one gets when using the design in the appendix.

11. David Roozen, William McKinney, and Jackson Carroll, *Varieties of Religious Presence* (New York: Pilgrim Press, 1984), suggests that congregations "hold the center" as I have described in this grid. That book also suggests, helpfully, that individual congregations may have different "centers." A congregation may have a central understanding of its message that could make the community itself focus in one of the quadrants. If so, the congregation's task would be to hold that center and provide a dependable reference point to which members could return for renewal of their special calling.

Chapter 4

1. Nomenclature is always a problem here. Each denomination has a different name for the structure that provides this organizational environment for individual congregations. I will use the awkward word that has become used by consensus: judicatory. I do so even as I harbor a few unkind thoughts of my Presbyterian colleagues who apparently coined the word and foisted it off upon us. The word is actually used for any level of the church structure outside the congregation, but I will use it almost exclusively for the regional organization of the church, not the national. Even the word regional is awkward. Some denominations have two levels of judicatory between congregations and national structures. Presbyterians have regionally small presbyteries and larger synods. Episcopalians have regionally close dioceses and vestigial provinces for larger areas. In this discussion I am talking about the close-by judicatory—the one in direct and regular contact with congregations.

2. See Loren B. Mead, *The Once and Future Church* (Washington, DC: The Alban Institute, 1991).

3. As a life-long Episcopalian who grew up with doctrines of apostolic succession as the basis for having bishops, I remember hearing the story of the early efforts of the Protestant Episcopal Church to send mission workers to Japan. In the story the early missionaries were perplexed at why the Japanese had a hard time understanding the denomination, until they had translated back to them the Japanese name for the church: The Society of Contradicting Overseers. Frankly, that's not a bad name for the way the house of bishops operates, but I'll defend them to the death!

4. A hot spot that has come to light in the nineties has been the role of the judicatory and the congregation in cases of sexual misbehavior on the part of the male pastor. The more "connectional" systems generally have more power to act to discipline the pastor than the denominations in which pastoral discipline is more heavily congregational. A pastor who has misbehaved, even misbehaved flagrantly, sometimes is able to maintain the fervent support of the congregation. Pastoral loyalty sometimes combines with blame-the-victim thinking to give some such pastors immunity.

5. This is a five-day educational event for those in the role of bishop or executive. Sponsored by The Alban Institute, this event is held

annually for three dozen or so people. Information is available at 1-800-486-1318.

6. Ghost Ranch in New Mexico is more familiarly known to northern Presbyterians as "heaven." Southern Presbyterians reserve that term for Montreat, North Carolina.

7. My staff colleague Speed Leas is one of the pioneers among church leaders in developing ways to work with and through conflicts. His writing, teaching, and wise counsel have helped dozens of conflicts turn to growth for the people involved. The potential for escalation always hits me humorously when I read the prayer found in many evening liturgies. How many churches have prayed this prayer? "O God, make Speed to save us!"

8. See Edwin Friedman, *Generation to Generation: Family Process in Church and Synagogue* (New York: Guilford Press, 1985), a prime resource for judicatory executives and bishops.

9. See Roy Oswald, *Clergy Self Care* (Washington, DC: The Alban Institute, 1991), and any other books by Oswald.

10. Two programs, both initially begun by the Lilly Endowment, Inc., try to address some of this. Operating out of Trinity Episcopal Church, 3242 N. Meridian St., Indianapolis, IN 46208, a nationwide effort (Trustee Leadership Program) is helping to develop congregational boards using models from nonprofit organizations and educational institutions. Chuck Olsen, a Presbyterian pastor, is also completing the Set Apart Lay Leader project to discover models and methods to help church-board leadership. Contact: Dr. Charles Olsen, 15003 NW Seventy-second St., Kansas City, MO 64512.

Chapter 5

1. See Loren B. Mead, *New Hope for Congregations* (New York: Seabury Press, 1972). This was my first attempt at "learning from our experience" in working with congregations. At that time most religious studies were of ideas, but some remarkable sociologists were trying to understand empirical dimensions of religious organizations. The story of the shift of energy in religious studies from deductive to inductive has only begun and has not yet been told.

2. I have more to say about a systems approach, but that will have to wait for my next book.

3. For details of this shift of consciousness, see Loren B. Mead, *The Once and Future Church* (Washington, DC: The Alban Institute, 1991).

4. If I had my wish, no student would graduate from seminary without having made three or four planned-giving visits to a prospective seminary donor.

5. I speak about my work with the founders of the Consortium of Endowed Episcopal Churches and the Presbyterian Network of Endowed Congregations. Each of these groups meets annually to share discoveries about how to minister effectively as congregations with sizable endowments. Attempts to develop similar networks in Unitarian-Universalist, United Methodist, and United Church of Christ denominations did not result in continuing dialogue. My work with all except the Episcopal group was supported by grants from the Lilly Endowment. See Loren B. Mead, *Endowed Congregations: Pros and Cons* (Washington, DC: The Alban Institute, 1990).

6. In building The Alban Institute, Inc., we have been conscious that we were working on this frontier. The characteristics of that institute—its focus on building accountability in relationships, searching for an alternate way to fund the delivery of skilled services within the religious world, the effort to develop a network of skilled people who live off the sale of their skills, and its monomaniacal focus on the life of the congregation—represent our reading of some of the characteristics needed in other institutions we need to be building for the future of the churches.

7. Verna Dozier's personal influence, preaching, and teaching lie behind my thinking.

8. Thomas Harris, *I'm O.K.—You're O.K.* (New York: Harper & Row, 1969). Although I will deal here with the unhealthy side of what Harris describes, note that his book also deals with the positive memories that childhood and parenting can bring.

9. One very practical application of this knowledge has been worked out by my colleague Speed Leas, a conflict-management consultant. In a conflict situation, the most parental and childish responses are frequently in command. Speed finds that one of the most helpful interventions is to "trigger the adult." He gives assignments that force the combatants to get out of childish or parental behavior: "Let us try to agree on a set of rules for how to carry out this conflict." Or, "Here are

the six steps I plan to carry out in working on this conflict with you. Can you suggest anything I have left out?" Frequently he gives combatants team assignments to gather data together—with people who oppose one another having to collaborate on a task that all agree needs to be done. We have found that the very presence of an outside consultant brings potential to increase adult-adult communication and checks the use of parent-child transactions.

10. To this day I am ashamed of the childish resentment I used to feel against one clergyman who exhorted me every Sunday to do this or do that when I was doing all I knew how to do; he never gave me any direction about how to do what he wanted. I sat there, emotionally sucking my thumb and thinking "You can't make me!" And I was no kid at the time.

11. See Mead, *The Once and Future Church*, ch. 5.

12. Several decades ago this was known as "morphological fundamentalism." The phrase is so absurd that I've loved it since I first saw it in the Western European working paper of the World Council of Churches' great study in the sixties: "The Missionary Structure of the Congregation." See *The Church for Others: Two Reports on the Missionary Structure of the Congregation* (Geneva: World Council of Churches, 1967).

13. Someone who will read this book remembers the time he asked me, "Is there anything that always causes conflict in a church?" I replied, "Yes. Try moving any of the furniture around." Three years later he phoned me, somewhat sheepishly, and said, "You were right. I wish we had listened. We need help with a fight that's broken out about moving the altar." They did a great job of working with the conflict. The altar was moved, but not as was first proposed, and they all lived happily ever after. Or at least for a decade or so. He first asked me that question nearly twenty years ago. I would still give the same answer.

14. That was a simple statement when I first made it. But during the period of rewriting this manuscript, we installed voice-mail at the office. I was astonished by my own rage at this new system that I knew was an improvement, that I helped decide was the right one for us, that I even helped raise the money to pay for. How terribly difficult it is to change. For anybody.

15. Kurt Lewin's wide influence as a theoretician about change, about human interaction, and about the nature of groups arose from a life

of teaching more than from systematic writing. I got most of my knowledge of these theories from those to whom he had taught them in semi-
nars and small group interactions. Some of his basic thinking is found in
the following books: *A Dynamic Theory of Personality* (New York and
London: McGraw Hill, 1935) and *Resolving Social Conflicts* (New York:
Harper, 1948).

   16. See Mead, *The Once and Future Church*, ch. 5. There I dealt
with some of these dynamics in terms of "learning points" and "accountability." I think the old joke about the guy slamming the mule with a
two-by-four "just to get his attention" is making the same point. If you
attempt to change something without getting their attention, forget it.
You are wasting time.

   17. Elisabeth Kubler-Ross, *On Death and Dying* (New York:
Macmillan, 1969).

   18. Stephen L. Fink, Joel Beak, and Kenneth Taddeo, "Organizational Crisis and Change," *Journal of Applied Behavioral Sciences* 7, no.
1: 15-37. We first became aware of this theory in 1975-76 when, with a
group of colleagues, Roy Oswald initiated studies about how institutions
and congregations could deal constructively with the financial crises and
down-sizing that was prevalent in those recessionary years. The theories
have become even more important as it has become clear that down-
sizing of religious institutional structures is not a matter of immediate
crisis but of a long-range change that has made crisis an intrinsic element
of the religious world.

   19. An extremely valuable addition to our knowledge has come
from the research of David M. Noer, *Healing the Wounds: Overcoming
the Trauma of Layoffs and Revitalizing Downsized Organizations* (San
Francisco: Jossey-Bass, 1993). Noer's work explores how firings effect
the survivors and makes a good case for the critical importance of attention to this neglected area of organizational development. Noer suggests a four-level model of intervention to help reorganization survivors
overcome their wounds and build constructive new work lives. Anyone
in a judicatory or national church office should have access to this
helpful book.

Appendix

1. David Roozen, William McKinney, and Jackson Carroll, *Varieties of Religious Presence* (New York: Pilgrim Press, 1984). See especially the graph on page 87. If you use this graph, point out that it is somewhat reversed from the one I have suggested. Also point out that their grid is graphing congregations, while the one I present is graphing people.

The Alban Institute:
an invitation to membership

The Alban Institute, begun in 1979, believes that the congregation is essential to the task of equipping the people of God to minister in the church and the world. A multi-denominational membership organization, the Institute provides on-site training, educational programs, consulting, research, and publishing for hundreds of churches across the country.

The Alban Institute invites you to be a member of this partnership of laity, clergy, and executives—a partnership that brings together people who are raising important questions about congregational life and people who are trying new solutions, making new discoveries, finding a new way of getting clear about the task of ministry. The Institute exists to provide you with the kinds of information and resources you need to support your ministries.

Join us now and enjoy these benefits:

CONGREGATIONS, The Alban Journal, a highly respected journal published six times a year, to keep you up to date on current issues and trends.

Inside Information, Alban's quarterly newsletter, keeps you informed about research and other happenings around Alban. Available to members only.

Publications Discounts:

- [ ] 15% for Individual, Retired Clergy, and Seminarian Members
- [ ] 25% for Congregational Members
- [ ] 40% for Judicatory and Seminary Executive Members

Discounts on Training and Education Events

Write our Membership Department at the address below or call us at 1-800-486-1318 or 301-718-4407 for more information about how to join The Alban Institute's growing membership, particularly about Congregational Membership in which 12 designated persons receive all benefits of membership.

 The Alban Institute, Inc.
Suite 433 North
4550 Montgomery Avenue
Bethesda, MD 20814-3341